Praise for
Lies, Damned Lies, and Science

"Comprehensive, readable, and replete with current, useful examples, this book provides a much-needed explanation of how to be a critical consumer of the scientific claims we encounter in our everyday lives."
— **April Cordero Maskiewicz**, Department of Biology, Point Loma Nazarene University

"This book treats a topic that is very important to any citizen: How to sort through the maze of information and interpretations that are put forward in the name of science. One of the most important institutions in society, science is often misunderstood and manipulated. Seethaler's book helps the reader look inside the workings of science and gain a deeper understanding of the pathway that is followed by a scientific finding—from its beginnings in a research lab to its appearance on the nightly news."
— **Jim Slotta**, Ontario Institute for Studies in Education, University of Toronto

"How I wish science was taught this way! Seethaler builds skills for critical thinking and evaluation. The book is rich with examples that not only illustrate her points beautifully; they also make it very interesting and fun to read."
— **Julia R. Brown**, Director, Targacept, Inc.

"Using accessible and engaging examples, Dr. Seethaler presents a clear framework for making sense of the science information we often receive incompletely through the popular media. This book is an important contribution toward the better understanding of and use of scientific knowledge in making decisions that impact our lives and our society."
— **Stephanie Sisk-Hilton**, Department of Elementary Education, San Francisco State University

"As Sherry Seethaler says herself, the book gives you tools to understand science, and she delivers them with simplicity, clarity, and wit. Seethaler helps us all decipher the Rosetta stones of modern science."
— **Raymond Hardie**, author of *Abyssos* and *Fleet*

Lies, Damned Lies, and Science

Lies, Damned Lies, and Science

How to Sort through the Noise around Global Warming, the Latest Health Claims, and Other Scientific Controversies

Sherry Seethaler

Vice President, Publisher: Tim Moore
Associate Publisher and Director of Marketing: Amy Neidlinger
Senior Acquisitions Editor: Amanda Moran
Editorial Assistant: Myesha Graham
Development Editor: Russ Hall
Digital Marketing Manager: Julie Phifer
Publicity Manager: Laura Czaja
Assistant Marketing Manager: Megan Colvin
Cover Designer: Stauber Design
Operations Manager: Gina Kanouse
Managing Editor: Kristy Hart
Project Editor: Anne Goebel
Copy Editor: Geneil Breeze
Proofreader: Water Crest Publishing
Indexer: Erika Millen
Senior Compositor: Gloria Schurick
Manufacturing Buyer: Dan Uhrig

© 2009 by Pearson Education, Inc.
Publishing as FT Press Science
Upper Saddle River, New Jersey 07458

FT Press Science offers excellent discounts on this book when ordered in quantity for bulk purchases or special sales. For more information, please contact U.S. Corporate and Government Sales, 1-800-382-3419, corpsales@pearsontechgroup.com. For sales outside the U.S., please contact International Sales at international@pearson.com.

Printed in the United States of America

ISBN-10: 0-13-284944-5
ISBN-13: 978-0-13-284944-9
Pearson Education LTD.
Pearson Education Australia PTY, Limited.
Pearson Education Singapore, Pte. Ltd.
Pearson Education North Asia, Ltd.
Pearson Education Canada, Ltd.
Pearson Educatión de Mexico, S.A. de C.V.
Pearson Education—Japan
Pearson Education Malaysia, Pte. Ltd.

Library of Congress Cataloging-in-Publication Data is on file.

This product is printed digitally on demand. This book is the paperback version of an original hardcover book.

For Barbara, who is amazing and wise

Contents at a Glance

Contents

Preface

Be very, very careful what you put into that head, because you will never, ever get it out.

—Thomas Cardinal Wolsey (1471-1530)

My goal in writing this book is to help people make sense of the science-related issues that impact their daily lives. *Lies, Damned Lies, and Science* provides an enlightening approach for contemplating scientific issues, and brings these issues into focus the way new glasses sharpen one's vision. In other words, the book is a new lens through which to view the world. Each chapter reveals a unique set of elements that need to be taken into consideration when reasoning about a complex science-related issue. In addition to bringing these elements into focus, the book shows how they fit together into something greater than a sum of parts.

Most of the messages that bombard us everyday are carefully selected to present just one of a kaleidoscope of possible perspectives on technological, environmental, economic, and health issues such as global warming, mad cow disease, nanotechnology, genetically engineered food, who should take cholesterol-lowering drugs, and what are the merits of banning plastic bags. Oversimplified black-and-white perspectives of issues come from those who have a vested interest in convincing others of their point of view, or who are simply relaying information without thinking critically about it. This book explores ways to achieve more nuanced and balanced perspectives on a wide range of issues.

In a society in which science and technology drive the economy and infiltrate every aspect of daily life, it is dangerous for an elite few to make the decisions about how technology is used, who will be given access to it, and how money is spent to research scientific solutions to societal problems. Ironically, those with the power to make these decisions rarely have any background in science. Therefore, they are especially vulnerable to being hoodwinked by those who hold stake in an issue and have the money to get their voices heard. Yet, we too can make our voices heard through sound, evidence-based political, consumer, and medical decisions. To do this, we need to be armed with the knowledge that makes it difficult for clever stakeholders to deceive us.

Too many people lost confidence in their ability to understand science because they did poorly in science class in high school. However, even folks who excelled in high school science classes and majored in a scientific discipline in college are rarely adequately prepared to think critically about the science they encounter in their daily lives. High school and even college science tends to be focused on facts, formulae, and experiments with known outcomes. In the real world, there is much more uncertainty and interpretation. Decisions about contemporary scientific issues often must be made on the basis of incomplete information, and conflicting viewpoints are the norm rather than the exception. This book unravels the complexity of such issues to help scientists and nonscientists alike identify hogwash and balance tradeoffs to make well-reasoned decisions about science in everyday life.

Introduction

Knowledge is power.

—Sir Francis Bacon (1561-1626)

If the words "xylem" and "phloem" bring to mind musical instruments rather than plants, and you could not tell a gastropod from an annelid if one turned up in your breakfast cereal, you are still perfectly capable of learning to see through the hype and hogwash that come your way. This book will give you something more powerful than facts. It will give you tools—the kind of tools that no one (not even the self-proclaimed science nerd) learned in school. The power of these tools is that they can be applied to any issue that arises. New facts will come to light over time, and old ones will be overturned, but these tools will last you a lifetime. They will help you interpret information that comes your way, and they will make it possible to pinpoint the relevant information that is missing from the discussion.

Science is omnipresent. We are surrounded by the fruits of the labors of scientists and engineers—from computers and cell phones to genetically engineered food to sportswear made from new types of fabric. Labels on snacks inform us that they are "all natural" or "reduced fat." Television commercials tell us to ask our doctor about medicines that can make us happier, more carefree, and full of energy. Headlines warn about the emergence and spread of new diseases. Our politicians hotly debate issues such as the regulation of stem cell research and what to do about global warming.

Consequently, science is central to an increasing number of the decisions we make each day. But while science is prevalent, the science-related information that comes to us is piecemeal and disconnected, often misleading, and sometimes dead wrong. To make matters worse, the textbook science we learn in school leaves us unprepared for grappling with complex contemporary scientific issues. Making science-related decisions in our daily lives requires more than the scientific "facts" we had to memorize and recall on tests. Sound decisions require the careful weighing of the pros and cons —tradeoffs—of each possible choice.

Every decision has tradeoffs. For this reason, we must be willing to challenge our politicians, lobbyists, marketers of consumer goods, proponents of the latest diet craze, and even our doctors. We should demand more balanced assessments of the impact of new legislation, the risks and benefits of new technologies, and the side effects of treatments for ailments. Unfortunately, our willingness to accept simple answers can make it easy for advertisers to pull the wool over our eyes, and make us deaf to the voices of dissenters when a clever-talking politician makes an action sound sensible and foolproof.

Lies, Damned Lies, and Science will empower people of all ages and educational backgrounds to think critically about science-related issues and make well-balanced decisions about them.

Those who promote incorrect information, either because they are trying to manipulate you, or because they themselves have been duped or are simply misinformed, rarely have more knowledge about science than you do. What they have are skills at using information to suit their purposes. Your strongest line of defense against them is the set of tools you will learn in this book. After reading *Lies, Damned Lies, and Science*, you will have a solid grasp of how scientific knowledge develops, a familiarity with the kinds of individuals and groups filtering the scientific information that comes your way, and an understanding of the multitude of ways in which they can hoodwink you. As you read each chapter, you will become increasingly impervious to the efforts of others to manipulate you with misinformation.

Each of the ten chapters in the book describes one tool and illustrates it through thought-provoking topics in health, the environment, and technology, including the genetic engineering of crops, mad cow disease, global warming, electromagnetic fields, and drug treatments for depression. Every chapter will take you one step closer to being a savvy scientific reasoner. The chapters reveal how to

1. Understand how science progresses and why scientists sometimes disagree.
2. Identify those who hold stake in an issue and what their positions are.
3. Elucidate all the pros and cons of a decision.
4. Place alternatives in an appropriate context to evaluate tradeoffs.

5. Distinguish between cause and coincidence.

6. Recognize how broadly the conclusions from a study may be applied.

7. See through the number jumble.

8. Discern the relationships between science and policy.

9. Get past the ploys designed to simply bypass logic.

10. Know how to seek information to gain a balanced perspective.

Chapter 1, "Potions, Plot, Personalities." Everyone who has done science experiments in high school or as a freshman in college knows that there is only one correct outcome for an experiment, so why would scientists disagree about scientific findings? Sadly, school science usually presents an unrealistic view of how science really progresses. It gives the impression that doing science is about completing a set of steps, akin to following a recipe. This perspective fails to help us reason about current issues in science—science in the making. Without understanding why there could be legitimate reasons for scientists to come to different conclusions, it is frustrating to hear that scientists disagree, or that they have changed their minds about science-based advice they gave in the past. By understanding how science works, especially the role of interactions among scientists in the progress of science, it becomes easier to understand why scientists have disputes, to make sense of what is actually being disputed, and to recognize when the media is deliberately hyping disputes between scientists for drama, or missing the dispute entirely.

Chapter 2, "Who's Who?" Environmentalists. Farmers. Stockholders. Starving people in the poorest nations. Politicians. Consumers. Scientists. Corporations. These are all groups that have something to gain or to lose from new technologies, new legislation, the funding of various types of research, or the oversight of certain industries. Identifying the different groups can provide order to the cacophony of stakeholders' voices. Also, some voices may be missing from the mix; individuals with the fewest resources are often unrepresented. Knowing who the possible stakeholders are for a particular scientific issue, and seeking out the positions and opinions of those who tend to be less successful at making themselves heard, is essential for coming to balanced decisions.

Chapter 3, "Decisions, Decisions." Stakeholders represent their positions in the best possible light by focusing on the positive and omitting mention of the possible negative consequences. Of course, a balanced decision is one that is made by sorting through all relevant options and assessing the pros and cons of each. Otherwise, if alternatives and possible consequences are omitted from consideration, a decision is essentially being made at random. It is not much more informed than drawing choices from a hat. Since stakeholders cannot be depended on to present the whole picture, it is essential to be familiar with the themes of tradeoffs that arise in decisions about science-related issues. Using knowledge about these themes of tradeoffs, you will be able to ask the right questions to get the full set of alternatives and possible outcomes to make an informed choice.

Chapter 4, "Compare and Contrast." Ideas can be misleading when they are taken out of the big picture context, or when something is evaluated without reference to its alternatives. Imagine someone said that he is from a place where a loaf of bread costs a nickel. To make that information meaningful, most people would automatically ask about the typical earnings of an individual from that place. However, too often when we receive information, we fail to ask, "compared to what?" For example, if the news tells us that a new surgical method has led to 3,000 deaths, we jump to the conclusion that the surgical method is dangerous. But dangerous relative to what? Does not having surgery to correct the illness lead to more deaths? What treatment was used previously, and how did patients fare with it? Considering issues in an appropriate context will help you accurately evaluate the pros and cons of a decision.

Chapter 5, "What Happens If...?" What is compelling proof that a nutritional supplement can boost the immune system, that human activities are changing global climate, or that a new technology is not deleterious to human health? Many claims are about a factor causing some result. The evidence offered in support of these claims ranges from the testimonials that bombard us everyday, "Product X changed my life," to the controlled scientific experiment. Despite what the plethora of claims may lead one to believe, it is difficult to prove that two things are linked by cause rather than coincidence. Delving into the strengths and weaknesses of the different types of evidence reveals when it is and is not possible to conclude that there is a causal link between two occurrences.

Chapter 6, "Specific or General." Data collected under one set of circumstances are often used to draw conclusions about different cir-cumstances. For example, conclusions may be drawn about the danger of a chemical to human health based on toxicity tests in animals. However, data collected with one population, in a specific location, under certain conditions, or at a particular epoch cannot necessarily be legitimately applied to other situations. Because stakeholders often apply conclusions much more widely than they should, it is critical to understand what kinds of problems can arise when findings are applied to novel situations.

Chapter 7, "Fun Figures." Many stakeholders will attempt to blind you with statistics. Used correctly, statistics can be informative, but more often than not, the numbers are inadvertently misleading or are deliberately being used to tell lies. Evaluating the statistics presented by stakeholders does not require sophisticated math skills. Instead, it is a matter of identifying the common pitfalls that arise when interpreting what the numbers mean, such as confounding factors, lack of significance, meaninglessness, and oddities in the way the data were collected.

Chapter 8, "Society's Say." Science is embedded in a greater social fabric. Society puts limitations on the kinds of experiments that can be performed by prohibiting experiments deemed unethical. The availability or lack of funding for certain types of research projects also impacts science. For example, following the attacks of September 11, 2001, and the anthrax mailings, scientists whose research had applications to the war on terrorism found it easier to get research funds. Science and society intersect in another way when questions arise about scientific issues that cannot be answered by science itself. These ethical and moral questions come into play when individuals and governments make decisions about scientific issues. Ethical and moral questions are not constrained to traditionally sensitive issues such as the use of stem cells from human embryos. Ethical concerns, including how much risk is acceptable and how taxpayer dollars should be spent, arise in debates about issues like the use of pesticides, nuclear power, space exploration, and how to tackle diseases that plague developing nations. To judge the soundness of new policies, it is important to understand what values were applied to develop them.

Chapter 9, "All the Tricks in the Book." We all want to believe that our brains sort through information in the most rational way possible. On the contrary, countless studies by psychologists, educators, and neurobiologists show that there are many foibles of human reasoning. Common weaknesses in reasoning exist across people of all ages and educational backgrounds. For example, confirmation bias is ubiquitous. People pay attention to information that supports their viewpoints, while ignoring evidence to the contrary. Confirmation bias is not the same as being stubborn, and is not constrained to issues about which people have strong opinions. Instead, it acts at a subconscious level to control the way we gather and filter information. Most of us are not aware of these types of flaws in our reasoning processes, but professionals who work to convince us of certain viewpoints study the research on human decision making to determine how to exploit our weaknesses to make us more susceptible to their messages. Becoming more aware of our own vulnerabilities stymies their efforts.

Chapter 10, "Fitting the Pieces Together." Making sense of an issue requires knowing when to ask questions, what questions to ask, and whom to ask. It is critical to take stock of the information presented, and determine what information is missing. For complex issues, information gathering is akin to peeling an onion; successive levels of understanding reveal themselves as one digs deeper for information. With practice, it becomes natural to move between these levels of understanding when reasoning about an issue. In doing so, what was once an impenetrable mass will reveal its various components. Building on the tools introduced in Chapters 1 through 9, Chapter 10 discusses the different levels of understanding that play a part in making sense of science-related issues. It also provides details about where to find information and the reliability of different sources of information.

Conclusion, "Twenty Essential Applications of the Tools." In this Information Age, lack of information is rarely a problem. Instead, the challenge is sifting through and making sense of mounds of information. The tools discussed in Chapters 1 through 10 facilitate the sorting and synthesis of information by focusing attention where it is needed most. They provide a framework that can organize what seems like hopeless complexity into a comprehensible set of ideas, useful for making decisions and integrating new ideas as they come along. The Conclusion lays out the ideas discussed in *Lies, Damned Lies, and Science* in a handy, easily referenced format that will facilitate sense making about new issues as they emerge.

1

Potions, plot, personalities: understand how science progresses and why scientists sometimes disagree

In the sixth Harry Potter book, *Harry Potter and the Half-Blood Prince*, Harry developed a flair for making potions by following instructions handwritten in the margins of his potions textbook by the book's previous owner. To make a Draught of Living Death, for instance, the handwritten notes in Harry's book advised him to stir his potion clockwise after seven stirs in the opposite direction. The tiny tweak in the procedure helped Harry achieve potion perfection. Meanwhile, Harry's brilliant friend, Hermione, who carefully followed the original textbook instructions line by line, became frustrated when she could not get her potions to turn out properly. Of course, at Hogwarts School of Witchcraft and Wizardry, potion making relies on magic. Surely, in a university laboratory outside J. K. Rowling's magical world, the synthesis of chemicals would not be affected by something as insignificant as how the chemicals are stirred? Surprisingly, when a published chemical reaction—the cleaving of bonds between carbon atoms—inexplicably stopped working, a frustrating eight-month investigation did indeed trace the problem to how the solution was stirred. Iron was leaching out of the well-used magnetic stir bar of the chemist who developed and published the chemical reaction. It turned out that the metal was important for catalyzing the reaction. Researchers attempting to replicate the reaction had unwittingly removed the catalyst because they were using a new stir bar with its metal core well sealed in its plastic casing. There was no need to invoke the supernatural to explain the mystery of the failed reaction—the findings were published in the sedate chemistry journal

Organometallics—but this example shows that science, like *Harry Potter*, has a plot with unexpected twists and turns. Because the science that comes to us in our daily lives is usually science-in-the-making, to make sense of it, it is essential to understand how science really progresses.

Brewing chemicals in a laboratory is a stereotype that comes to mind when we hear the word "scientist," but scientists actually engage in a wide range of activities. Many scientists—for example, ecologists, archeologists, climatologists, and geologists—spend much of their time doing field research. This may involve documenting the behavior of animals in the wild to understand population declines, collecting ice cores in Antarctica and using gas bubbles trapped within them to gain information about changes in the earth's atmosphere over time, or recording seismic activity near volcanoes or fault lines.

Of course, scientists often do spend considerable time in a laboratory, but the work they do there differs depending on several factors. Some of these include: whether the laboratories are affiliated with universities, hospitals, companies, zoos, or the government; how many scientists work there; how much funding they have; what kinds of research questions they focus on; what kind of equipment is used; and even where the labs are located. For example, physicists who study neutrinos—one of the fundamental particles that make up the universe—use special laboratory facilities a mile or more beneath the earth's surface.

It should come as no surprise, then, that despite what most science textbooks may lead you to believe, there is no single method of doing science. This is one of three aspects of science frequently misrepresented by precollege and even college science courses. The second problem with these courses is that they leave the learner with the impression that science is merely an accretion of new ideas. However, in reality, controversy and revolutions in scientific thought are common features of science. Third, despite stereotypes of scientists as loners, interactions between scientists play many important roles in the progress of science. This chapter dispels the myths about these aspects of scientific progress and reveals how dispelling each myth can make one a more critical consumer of the claims about science that come through the media and other sources.

"The scientific method"—not as easy as pi

Introductory science textbooks often lay out a neat set of steps they refer to as "the scientific method" and leave readers with the impression that this is all they need to know about how science is done. The steps most texts describe can be summarized more or less as follows:

1. Develop a hypothesis.
2. Design an experiment to test the hypothesis.
3. Perform the experiment and collect data.
4. Analyze the data collected.
5. Decide if the data support or refute the hypothesis.

This view of science is oversimplified, incomplete, and sets people up for failure when they try to make sense of science in the real world. While it might be reasonable to give children a simplified view of science to begin with, the problem is that many people, even college students who major in science, never get to see what authentic science is like. With some notable exceptions, undergraduate science laboratories are cookbook exercises, and undergraduate lecture courses are just that—lectures, usually more about presenting facts to be memorized than discussing how those facts came to be. For those who go on to graduate school in the sciences, it is often a shock when it takes months to figure out why experiments are not working, that what initially seemed to be an exciting result is an error, or (for the lucky ones) that what seemed to be an error turns out to be an exciting result.

The process of testing hypotheses is not nearly as cut-and-dried as the textbook scientific method would lead one to believe. First, multiple hypotheses are possible, but the one that ultimately stands up to the test may not be apparent from the start. It may only be proposed after several other hypotheses have been eliminated. Second, there may be more than one type of experiment that can be done to test a hypothesis, and each possible experimental test will have its own set of pros and cons. These include time and cost required, expected accuracy of the results, feasibility of applying the results to other situations, ease of acquiring the necessary equipment, and amount of training needed to use that equipment. Then again, the tools or techniques required to rigorously test the hypothesis may not exist. For example, geologists cannot physically probe the center of the earth. Instead they must make inferences about it based on seismic data. Third, data analysis is rarely simple and straight-forward. Decisions must be made about whether to include data that appear spurious, what to do if experimental subjects dropped out of an experiment before it was over, and, as discussed in the next section, how to interpret data that was collected using new technologies. Finally, it may be possible to draw more than one conclusion from the same data. For example, if multiple factors can each play a role in causing some-thing, it will likely take more than one experiment to tease them apart. A discussion of these caveats of designing experiments and interpreting data is usually absent from media reports about science.

With new tools, researchers can answer new questions—but only after the bugs are worked out

Over time, as new technologies develop, scientists can begin to test hypotheses they could not have tested in the past. But for the conclu-sions drawn from experiments using new procedures or new technolo-gies to be accepted by the scientific community, other scientists must agree that the new technique does measure the effect of interest, and that what is being "observed" is real.

For example, chemists often want to know the structure of particular molecules. This information is used in many ways, including drug design. One way to determine a molecule's structure is Nuclear Magnetic Reso-nance (NMR). NMR relies on the fact that when a molecule is placed in a magnetic field and probed using radio waves, the behavior of the nucleus of each atom depends on the identity of its neighboring atoms. A chemist can load a vial containing a sample of the molecules of interest into an NMR machine and get a graph that consists of a series of peaks. The structure of the molecule is inferred from this graph. The key word is "inferred." The chemist operates on the assumption that the peaks cor-respond to atoms, and are not some artifact of the procedure like electri-cal surges or vibrations in the room.

NMR is a well-accepted experimental technique used everyday by scientists all over the world. For a technique like NMR to become accepted, it must withstand a series of tests. For instance, if an older technique measures the same thing (presumably less efficiently), then the output of the new technique can be compared to that of the old. Alternatively, researchers can study the output of the new technique when it is used to analyze a set of known standards. For a new NMR technique, scientists could take chemicals that have a known molecular structure, run NMRs, and have other scientists, who did not know what the original samples were, interpret the graphs. If this can be done accurately and consistently over a wide range of samples, the technique can be used to identify unknown samples.

Even when the procedure or technology has been used for a time in one context, or to collect one type of data, applying it to collect another type of data, or to collect data under different conditions, may lead to disputes about what is really being observed. For example, a test that measures the concentration of a specific chemical may work well when the solution being tested is simple. On the other hand, when many other chemicals are present, they may participate in side reactions that interfere with the analysis. So the test may give accurate readings for well water or lake water, but may give false readings when applied to the analysis of blood samples or industrial waste. For this reason, new applications of procedures require careful consideration and verification.

Furthermore, although scientists may agree with each other on what they are observing with a given procedure, they may not agree on what the observations mean. For example, some brain scans allow scientists to measure blood flow to different regions of the brain. By studying changes in blood flow when people engage in different tasks—such as solving jigsaw puzzles, listening to music, memorizing a list of words—scientists infer what regions of the brain are necessary for those tasks. But an increase in blood flow does not necessarily mean that region of the brain is "thinking." Other scientists could accept that the scan is indeed measuring blood flow, while arguing that the increase in blood flow means that more messages are being sent through that region of the brain, rather than being processed there, or that the blood flow is due to an increase in cell maintenance and repair that occurs after a region of the brain has finished thinking. They might suggest further tests of the technique to address their concerns.

Uncertainty about what tool or procedure to use, and the risk that results are not what they appear to be, are problems common to all the scientific disciplines. The development of new tools allows scientists to answer questions they could not answer in the past, and the answers to those questions will lead to new questions, and so on. Therefore, new technologies and procedures are crucial to the progress of science. At the same time, other scientists unfamiliar with a new tool may express skepticism and call for others to replicate the experiments. Because this skepticism often comes to us in the form of sound bites, and because uncertainty about experimental tools is an aspect of science that is not familiar to most people, even people with a bachelor's degree in science, the skepticism may seem like waffling. Waffling is annoying when you are trying to make decisions on the basis of the scientific information that comes your way. However, if a new technique is the source of the uncertainty, time and future experiments will confirm or disconfirm its usefulness and clear up uncertainty.

Myth #1

Science is a step-by-step process in which scientists develop a hypothesis, design an experiment to test it, perform the experiment, collect data, analyze the data, and accept or refute the hypothesis based on it.

Not exactly. If science really were so straightforward, hypotheses would not remain untested for long periods of time. Scientists would not disagree about results.

Implications for making sense of scientific issues:

A basic understanding of the challenges scientists face in testing hypotheses takes the mystery out of why hypotheses remain untested and why scientists disagree. For example, new experimental techniques make it possible to test hypotheses that could not be tested in the past. At the same time, new experimental techniques must hold up to scrutiny before the scientific community will accept the results collected using them. Discord about an experimental technique should not be treated as the sign of an impasse. Instead, the results should be taken into consideration, but decisions based on the results collected using the technique should be conservative until the technique has been rigorously tested.

Models play a critical role in the progress of science

Volcanoes are a real hit with kids. Build a hollow, cone-shaped structure from some simple household items, throw in some vinegar, red food dye, and baking soda, and whoosh—the eruption makes a big, foaming mess.

Of course, while these science fair model volcanoes bear a superficial resemblance to real volcanoes, they function in a completely different way. Obviously, scientists looking for a system on which to conduct laboratory tests to better understand volcanic eruptions would not turn to the popular science fair volcano. This highlights a critical feature that distinguishes the kinds of models that were used to teach us science and the kinds of models that scientists use to understand the world. On the one hand, teachers and parents use model volcanoes to create excitement and give young students a physical object to which they can tie the earth science concepts they are learning. Likewise, a teacher may use ping pong balls to show how molecules of a gas bounce off each other and the sides of a container. For the purpose of helping students understand difficult scientific concepts, it does not matter that real magma behaves very differently than baking soda and vinegar, or that ping pong balls do not really mimic the behavior of gas molecules. These models make science more visual and are practical teaching tools. On the other hand, if the goal is to use a model to test hypotheses about how things work in the real world, the features of an ideal model are very different. In that case, the model does not have to look like its real world counterpart; it just has to act like it. For example, to understand what is happening in a cell when it switches between different types of fuel (carbohydrate, fat, protein), a plastic model of the cell showing all of the cell's organelles is completely inadequate. Considerably more useful is a computer program that simulates all of the major processes and chemical reactions in the cell.

Scientists use many different types of models, but in recent decades as computers have become increasingly powerful, computer simulations have become essential tools for scientists studying all kinds of complex systems. For example, computational models are used to understand the biological processes occurring within organisms, the functioning of ecosystems of organisms, the evolution of the universe, and climate changes. One kind of computer simulation is like the simulations used to make special effects in movies and computer games in that it aims to create a visual representation of reality (or unreality, in the case of some games and movies). Scientists use these kinds of simulations, for example, to determine the three-dimensional structure of proteins that play a role in different diseases. Knowing the structure of a protein makes it feasible to design a drug that can bind to the protein and modify its function. The second type of computer simulation is considerably more abstract and mathematical. Its output may not visually represent reality at all. Instead, it is used to determine what may occur given a specific set of initial conditions. Will the death of a star of a certain size give rise to a black hole? Given certain patterns of use of a new antibiotic, how long will it take before bacteria that are resistant to that antibiotic become widespread? How many degrees will global temperatures rise if we continue to emit greenhouse gases at the current rate?

Discussions in the media about global climate change frequently mention climate models, and "model-bashing" is a favorite pastime of climate change skeptics. The term "climate model" may bring to mind the familiar television weather map with its movements of air masses, clouds, and precipitation, but climate models are more mathematical and complex than weather forecasts. Rather than predicting the movements of air masses a few days in advance (which is a challenge in itself—no matter what the Weather Channel says, pack an umbrella just in case), climate models deal with larger regions over longer time scales. A considerable number of factors (in scientific lingo—parameters) must be included in climate models. What are the patterns of greenhouse gas emissions, and what quantity of greenhouse gases can be expected to accumulate during the time period under consideration? How much will each greenhouse gas (carbon dioxide, methane, water vapor, and so on) contribute to warming? How will the increase in concentration of water vapor in the atmosphere affect cloud formation? How will the clouds influence temperature? What will be the concentration of atmospheric particles like soot that can act as seeds to trigger cloud formation? What other effects will the atmospheric particles have? How significantly will the warming reduce ice and snow cover, and how much will the resulting decrease in reflectivity further enhance the heating at the earth's surface? How will the uptake of carbon dioxide by plants and the ocean be affected by warming? How could the warming predictions be affected by other natural sources of climate variation, such as cyclic variations in the sun's output or volcanic activity on Earth? Whew!

The need to take all of these different parameters into account means that climate models require tremendous computational power. Supercomputers are often used to do the number crunching. In addition, developing the climate model is not simply a matter of devising mathematical equations to account for each parameter. None of the values of the parameters is known for certain, and each is the focus of ongoing research. As new data become available, models are updated accordingly. Models must also be tested. The models are used to make predictions about the world, and then refined based on their ability to mimic reality. As a result, models improve with time and further research. Current climate models are better than past models, but because so many factors are still uncertain, predictions of future temperature increases vary widely. The range of these predictions will likely narrow as each of the parameters becomes better understood.

Myth #2

Scientific models are visual representations of reality.

Not usually. Scientists may use models that are scaled down (for example, of the solar system) or scaled up (for example, of a molecule) versions of reality. However, these kinds of models are mostly used for explanatory and teaching purposes. The most important scientific models are those used to make and test predictions about the world.

Implications for making sense of scientific issues:

Biological, meteorological, geological, and other phenomena are highly complex and influenced by large numbers of interacting factors. As a result, predictions made about them are usually given as a range of possibilities, rather than as a single number. The predictions made through modeling should be interpreted with caution but not dismissed just because there is uncertainty associated with them. Scientific models are refined based on how well they can predict the behavior of things in the real world; therefore, models are constantly improving.

What's all this talk about controversy?

In school, students rarely learn to view disagreements among scientists as a natural part of the progress of science; most textbooks are written as if science is a set of truths to be memorized. Teachers, especially in

America, are under enormous pressure to cover a large number of unrelated science topics each year to prepare their students for accountability tests, which generally measure students' ability to recall facts. When breadth is emphasized over depth, there simply is not time to discuss how the scientific ideas came to be. There is barely time to help students grasp the meaning of the ideas themselves. On the rare occasions when students are exposed to historical ideas about science, those ideas tend to be dismissed with minimal discussion of why they were replaced, or why scientists held them in the first place. Students are left with the impression that scientists held some silly ideas in the past, but now they have it all figured out, and today's scientific theories are true.

For folks who have never had the opportunity to learn how disagreements between scientists play a role in the progress of science, it can be confusing or frustrating to be told that scientists disagree about the meaning of a finding, or to find out that scientific advice they had taken to heart (eat margarine instead of butter) has been overthrown (avoid margarine—it's bad for you). However, controversy within science has always been a normal part of the progress of science. Familiarity with past examples of clashes between scientists can help one better understand the science-in-the-making in the media today. The historical example of what came to be the foundational theory on which modern geology is built, though initially proposed by one scientist and rejected by nearly all of his contemporaries, provides insight into how and why revolutions in scientific thinking occur.

Scientific revolutions really happen

In 1912, Alfred Wegener formulated a hypothesis about continental drift. The basic idea of continental drift is that all of the earth's landmasses were once joined together as a supercontinent, Pangaea, which later broke apart, leaving the continents gliding across the substratum. Wegener had several lines of evidence to support his continental drift hypothesis. The outlines of the continents look more or less as though they should fit together like pieces of a jigsaw. The distributions of living things, past and present, have striking similarities on different continents. There are similarities in rock formations on different continents. The distribution of climates was not the same a few hundred million years ago as it is today. Continental drift is an elegant hypothesis that can explain many puzzling observations. Yet many scientists gave it two thumbs down for nearly half a century.

The problem was that Wegener had no plausible mechanism for how continents could drift. It would take huge amounts of energy to move something as massive as a continent, no matter how slowly. How on earth could the continents be moving? Understanding mechanism is a big part of science, and scientists frown on "hand-waving" sorts of explanations, which is all Wegener could come up with based on the data available to him. Wegener himself recognized the gaps in his ideas and acknowledged them in his writing.

Ultimately, it was new data that drove the acceptance of continental drift. Three discoveries were pivotal. First, scientists discovered that the rocks on the ocean floor are much younger than the rocks that make up the continents. Second, they found a long chain of mountains, with active volcanoes along its middle and ancient volcanoes bordering them, that forms a continuous north-south seam in the middle of the Atlantic Ocean. Third, they discovered that there is a pattern of magnetic stripes with alternating polarity—some with their north pole facing north and some with their north pole facing south—along the ocean floor, parallel to the mountain chain beneath the Atlantic. Scientists already knew that, as it cools, molten rock laid down by volcanoes becomes magnetized according to the orientation of the earth's magnetic field, and that the earth's magnetic field has reversed itself several times throughout history. Therefore, the magnetic stripes on the ocean floor suggested that magnetized, solidified rock was pushed aside as new rock—which may have a different magnetic orientation depending on the orientation of the earth's magnetic field at the time—was laid down by volcanic activity. These results are consistent with the idea that volcanic activity between adjacent continental plates caused Pangaea to break apart about 200 million years ago, forming the Atlantic Ocean. The continents on either side of the ocean are still being pushed apart as the Atlantic Ocean widens by a couple inches per year.

Wegener died during a research expedition to Greenland in 1930, about three decades before his ideas about continental drift revolutionized geology. In fact, much of the research that led to key findings about sea floor magnetic stripes and spreading had nothing to do with testing continental drift. The research was going on in the 1950s, during the Cold War, when the United States hoped that studying the sea floor would provide information that would allow it to disguise its own submarines and better detect the Soviet Union's submarines. The nearly universal acceptance of continental drift resulted from the research of many scientists, working in different places on different projects. Eventually, as the pieces came together, the critique of Wegener's ideas as "preposterous" no longer made sense. It was more preposterous to maintain that the arrangement of oceans and continents was immutable in the face of the overwhelming evidence in support of continental drift.

This account of continental drift leaves out work done since the 1960s. The later work has led to a more detailed theory known as **plate tectonics**, which subsumes continental drift and includes much more detail about the forces that drive the movements of the plates. Nonetheless, the lesson is clear. The clash of ideas is not a problem in science, but rather a normal part of scientific progress. In the face of new evidence, a crazy idea can become the foundation for work in a field. It may take time for the evidence to accumulate, especially if tools are not available to test a hypothesis directly, but in the end, it is the data that do the talking.

Disputes are not a sign of science gone wrong

Because people tend to think of science as a slow accretion of ideas, where discord has no place, the existence of disagreements between scientists has been used to attack the theory of evolution. For example, at one point, existing paleontological (fossil) evidence and molecular (genetic) evidence told different stories about from which animals whales had evolved. The genetic evidence suggested that whales and hippopotami were closely related and shared a common ancestor. According to the fossil evidence available at the time, whales and hippos were only distantly related. Antievolutionists pointed to this disagreement as a flaw in science and a reason for rejecting evolutionary theory. At the same time, the paleontologists and molecular biologists were far from satisfied by the lack of agreement between the two types of data. They came up with explanations for why each might be inaccurate. Paleontologists criticized the molecular evidence because genetics cannot be used to compare the many species that have gone extinct, only the living examples of related species (except in rare cases in which well-preserved DNA from extinct species is available). Molecular biologists criticized the fossil evidence as being insufficient because a small percentage of organisms become fossilized and of those that do and are unearthed, the limb bones may not be well preserved. However, there is a significant difference between the approach of the antievolutionists and the scientists. Unlike the antievolutionists, the scientists specified what would be convincing support for one position or the other. In addition, the scientists predicted that the controversy would be resolved when additional evidence, either molecular evidence or fossil evidence, came to light.

Paleontologists eventually discovered fossils of ancient whales that had hind limbs. The hind limbs contained ankle bones that were clearly similar to those of hippopotami and their close relatives. Therefore, the new fossil finds brought the fossil evidence and the genetic evidence on whale evolution into agreement. This example shows that pointing to discord between scientists as indicative of a weakness in science is misguided. Scientists point out discord themselves. They seek evidence that will help them resolve the discord. Discord arises because science is a work in progress. The scientific process is healthy when scientists are willing to reconsider their ideas in the light of new evidence. While it is completely sensible to draw attention to discord to highlight where more research is needed, it is not sensible to use discord between scientists as a reason to throw one's hands in the air and give up on science.

Living organisms, earth processes, and the evolution of the universe are so complex that the existence of discord in science should not be puzzling. Even problems that seem straightforward, such as the relationship between estrogen levels and hot flashes, invariably turn out to be more complex when investigated thoroughly. Many women experience hot flashes—a feeling of intense heat often accompanied by flushing and sweating and sometimes followed by chills—as they approach and transition through menopause. Since estrogen levels decrease at menopause, and since estrogen supplements alleviate hot flashes, it is logical to assume that low estrogen levels trigger hot flashes. Some studies are consistent with this hypothesis, but others are not. While considered the hallmark of the menopausal transition, hot flashes can occur at other times of life and can affect both women and men. In addition, not all women experience hot flashes during menopause. Plus, some women who have low estrogen levels—for example, gymnasts or endurance athletes—do not experience hot flashes. These conflicting data have forced researchers to reconsider the role of estrogen in hot flashes. They hypothesize that hot flashes may not be triggered by low estrogen, but rather by estrogen levels that are in the process of declining. In other words, the cause may be the change in estrogen levels (dynamic) over time, not the absolute (static) level of estrogen at any point in time. Gathering the data to test the new hypothesis is trickier than gathering the data to test the original hypothesis. It requires following women over time to determine how their estrogen levels change and how the changes influence hot flashes. Long-term studies are expensive, time consuming, and challenging. In addition, other hormones and health and lifestyle factors likely play a role in who gets hot flashes. Since many experiments are needed to tease apart the complexities of an issue like the relationship between estrogen and hot flashes, it would be more surprising if conflicting ideas never arose in science and each new factoid was simply added on top of a pile of existing knowledge.

Myth #3

Science is the progressive accumulation of new facts.

No. If it were this simple, new information would accumulate, but old ideas would not be overthrown. In fact, revolutions in scientific thought do take place.

Implications for making sense of scientific issues:

We should base our decisions on today's scientific knowledge because it is the very best we have, collected with the most powerful tools available, and rooted in the work of generations of scientists. However, we must keep our minds open to the possibility that policies and courses of action may need to be altered in the face of contradictory evidence.

The media often misrepresents disputes between scientists

Disagreements between scientists are a normal part of the process of science, but the media often exaggerates, misrepresents, or oversimplifies these disputes to sensationalize the latest science news. This is especially common in headlines or brief sound bites. For example, there is new and still disputed evidence that moderate amounts of sun exposure may reduce a person's chances of getting certain internal cancers like breast, endometrial, colon, and prostate cancer. It is not hard to imagine the headlines and sound bites proclaiming, "scientists now say sun is good for you!"

Let's dissect this claim. On the surface, one could argue that it is accurate: Anything that reduces your risk of getting cancer is good. However, everyone knows that too much sun exposure can lead to skin cancer. So are scientists now disputing that? No. Is it possible that sun exposure could increase your risk of skin cancer, but decrease your risk of some internal cancers? Yes. Ultraviolet light from the sun can cause skin cancer by damaging DNA in skin cells, and this can ultimately cause cells to start multiplying out of control. Cancer is the result of the uncontrolled proliferation of cells. The proposed mechanism by which sun exposure might protect you from internal cancers is completely different. Exposure to the sun allows your body to synthesize vitamin D, and possibly other important compounds. Vitamin D, among other functions, may help prevent overproliferation of cells.

One obvious question is why sun exposure does not protect you from skin cancer if vitamin D can stop cells from proliferating out of control. It may be that the risk of bombarding the DNA in your skin cells with ultraviolet radiation from the sun outweighs the benefit of having a little extra vitamin D around. On the other hand, the sun's UV rays do not penetrate all the way through your skin, so your internal organs could benefit from the protective effects of extra vitamin D without the negative effects of UV radiation on their DNA.

For at least three reasons, this debate is much more complex than the headline might lead one to believe. First, scientists are still disputing whether it is true that sun exposure can protect you from internal cancers. The evidence for the claim is epidemiological data—the comparison of disease rates in different populations—which is useful but has many weaknesses. People who live in places where they get more sun likely have other lifestyle differences, such as diet and exercise, than their cold weather-dwelling counterparts. Second, even if the claim holds up, there still remains a tradeoff between increasing your risk of skin cancer while decreasing your risk of internal cancers. Third, those who believe sun exposure may protect you from internal cancers are not encouraging people to fry themselves in the sun. The body tightly controls vitamin D synthesis, and maximal synthesis may come after as little as 10 minutes in the sun, depending on the latitude, time of year, and your skin tone. So synthesizing enough vitamin D might be feasible without a significant increase in the risk of skin cancer. At this time, the jury is still out.

This example reveals the weaknesses of relying on sound bites as news. The headline "scientists now say the sun is good for you," might be used by some as a reason to lie out longer at the beach and/or to stop bothering to use sunscreen. On delving deeper into the evidence, it becomes clear these reactions would not be merited *even if* the relationship between sun exposure and reduced risk of internal cancers had been proven beyond a shadow of a doubt. Headlines and sound bites may give the impression that the disputing scientists share little common ground, when in fact, the dispute is often much more specific. In this example, the benefit of sun exposure in preventing internal cancers is under dispute; the risk of skin cancer from sun exposure is not. In the previous example, the scientists were not disputing that evolution occurred or that whales evolved from land animals; only what specific land animal is ancestral to whales was under dispute. Therefore, it is important to determine the extent of the disagreement between scientists before drawing conclusions about claims.

Another problem is what sociologist Christopher Toumey referred to as **pseudosymmetry of scientific authority**—the media sometimes presents controversy as if scientists are evenly divided between two points of view, when one of the points of view is held by a large majority of the scientific community. For example, until recently, the media often gave equal time and space to the arguments for and against humans as the cause of global climate change. Surveys of individual climate scientists have indicated that there is discord among scientists on the issue, but that the majority of scientists agree that humans are altering global climate. One analysis of a decade of research papers on global climate change found no papers that disputed human impacts on global climate. Also, all but one of the major scientific organizations in the United States whose members have expertise relevant to global climate change, more than a dozen organizations in all, have issued statements acknowledging that human activities are altering the earth's climate. The American Association of Petroleum Geologists dissents. Therefore, there is a general consensus within the scientific community that humans are causing global climate change. While it is legitimate to explore the arguments against the consensus position on global climate change, it is misleading for the media to present the issue so as to give the impression that the scientific community is evenly divided on the matter.

Myth #4

Disputes between scientists are an indication that there is a problem with the scientific process.

Not at all. It is normal and healthy for scientists to challenge each other's methods and conclusions.

Implications for making sense of scientific issues:

If disagreements between scientists are viewed as a breakdown of the scientific process, then it is easy to say, "scientists don't know anything anyway," and stop engaging in sense making. Beware of anyone who uses the fact that scientists disagree to denigrate science. On the other hand, if you hear "scientists now think…" you should wonder whether there is still controversy. What do the scientists agree on and what is still up for dispute? Headlines often misrepresent controversy, either inventing controversy where there essentially is none, or brushing over controversy to make a definitive statement when a more cautious statement is more appropriate. When trying to make a decision about voting, health care, nutrition, buying a new car, and so on, it is important to go beyond these sound bites to determine what is and is not under dispute.

From watering hole to prime time—birth and development of an idea

Interactions between scientists, and not just disputes, play a key role in the progress of science. However, nonscientists rarely are privy to the interactions between scientists, and scientists are often stereotyped as loners. Most everyone has heard a story about a scientist coming up with some amazing insight out of the blue. Probably the most famous such story was about Archimedes leaping from his bath, and running naked through the streets shouting, "Eureka!" (I have found it!) As the story goes, he had been looking for a way to help the king determine whether his new crown was made of pure gold, or if an unscrupulous jeweler had duped him by incorporating some amount of a lesser metal. Archimedes noticed the water overflowing as he got into his bath, and it occurred to him that an object submerged in water displaces a volume of water equal to the volume of the object. He also realized that a gold crown would have a smaller volume than a crown of equal mass constructed of a less dense metal like silver, or an alloy of gold and silver. So if the crown displaced more water than would an equal mass of gold, the king had been duped. Archimedes was so excited about his discovery that he forgot his tush was bare.

Scientists rarely work in isolation

Whether the story about Archimedes' eureka moment is true or not, it does reflect the stereotype of the brilliant scientist working alone to come up with a solution to a problem. Many scientists, and nonscientists alike, experience these sorts of "ah ha" moments while lost in their own reflections, sometimes even when they are taking a shower. Fortunately, not too many of them feel compelled to run around in their birthday suits proclaiming it to the world. However, while scientists work individually on certain tasks, they rarely do their work entirely in isolation. Neither folklore, nor textbooks, nor the media give much insight into the many levels of interactions among scientists that are so vital to the progress of science.

One form of interaction is informal brainstorming with colleagues. Like everyone else, scientists like to sit around and chew the fat. While a lot of this talk has nothing to do with science, not infrequently the conversation will get around to someone's current research project, and the brainstorming will begin. It may explore what the results of an experiment mean, what experiment to try next, or even something as banal as where to procure a necessary device or chemical. If there is a whiteboard, blackboard, or chart paper in the room, it will soon be covered with words, graphs, pictures, and formulae. Lack of a surface to write on is no deterrent. Napkins, backs of envelopes, and paper placemats will do the trick, and if restaurant crayons are the only writing implements available, so be it. The written artifacts resulting from the discussion will simply be more colorful. Bouncing ideas off colleagues is a great way to get a fresh perspective on one's own research because, after focusing on a problem for a while, it is sometimes hard to see the forest for the trees. Also, since individual scientists read different papers and attend different lectures and conferences, they may come across research potentially relevant to their colleagues. Furthermore, in other phases of science, scientists are expected to have sufficient evidence to back up their claims, but brainstorming with colleagues is an opportunity to get feedback on the hunches and crazy ideas that can sometimes end up revolutionizing a field. Exciting new ideas emerge when a bunch of bright people get together, listen to each other, and ask "what if?"

These informal discussions between scientists are so important that science buildings are often designed with common "watering holes," where people go for coffee breaks or to wait for an experiment to run to completion. Different labs may share this common area, and, when feasible, buildings are planned to place research groups with complementary research interests in proximity of each other. Of course, collaboration among colleagues is not restricted to science. Many businesses design space to facilitate informal interactions among employees, recognizing that this stimulates innovation.

Answering complex scientific questions also requires more formal interactions among people with different types of expertise. For example, determining how acid rain is affecting a forest would require a biologist who knows about plant metabolism and is able to gauge the health of the trees, and a chemist who understands how chemicals in the soil (for example, metals) react under acidic conditions and is able to perform tests on soil chemistry. A geologist's input about the types of rocks found in the area would also be valuable because different rocks (for example, limestone versus granite) are composed of different chemicals, which react differently with acid. It is therefore common for interdisciplinary teams of scientists to work together on grant proposals, projects, and papers. Even when scientists do not work together from the start of an investigation, a published study that identifies a problem—such as a new disease afflicting trees—may lead another scientist to build on the work by trying to gain insight into a possible contributing factor to that problem—such as changes in soil chemistry.

Scientists also constantly rely on tools and procedures that have been developed by other scientists. When scientists publish their results, they must carefully describe how they did the research. Published procedures are important to the progress of science because they ensure that scientists do not have to reinvent the wheel each time they want to do a new experiment. Perfecting experimental procedures is challenging and time consuming. For example, it may take months for a team of researchers to determine how to culture—grow—cells in the laboratory. Many different factors must be optimized. The cells will require special nutrients, as well as hormones and other chemicals that they would normally be exposed to in the body. Trial and error is used to determine the ideal composition of the culture medium—broth—to keep the cells healthy. Even the plates used to grow the cells must be perfected. The cells may not grow unless the plates are coated with a substance to which the cells can adhere. Finding a substance that is nontoxic and facilitates normal cell growth and division may also require trial and error. By publishing the composition of the culture medium and plate coating that promotes healthy cell growth and division, the researchers save other researchers countless hours of work, and make the scientific process much more efficient. It is not because of altruism that the researchers who do all the work to perfect a procedure make it available to everyone else. When the researchers publish a paper describing a procedure, it will be referenced in the papers of everyone who uses it. The publication of papers that are influential helps the researchers gain promotions, awards, and research funding.

Critique is very important in the publication process

While a scientist is coming up with a hypothesis to test, developing a way to test the hypothesis, and interpreting the results, close-working colleagues will provide cycles of review and feedback. Colleagues propose alternative hypotheses. They provide advice about how best to test the hypothesis, or help troubleshoot if technical difficulties arise with the experimental procedure or equipment. They suggest alternative ways of analyzing the data, such as more rigorous statistical tests. They may disagree with the conclusions drawn from the data and suggest other experiments that could be used to distinguish between alternative conclusions. If the findings hold up to scrutiny at this internal review level, then they are ready for the critical eye of outside scientists. In an academic setting—a university or other not-for-profit research center—scientists are expected to present their work at conferences and publish in peer-reviewed journals. "Publish or perish" is what young researchers are told. Scientists working in industry may also publish papers or present their results at scientific conferences, but industry scientists are often forced to keep critical aspects of their results private to protect proprietary knowledge, such as what chemicals and procedures are used to make a product or what compounds show promise toward becoming the next blockbuster drugs.

Results presented at scientific conferences are usually more preliminary than those presented in peer-reviewed journals. To give a talk at a conference, scientists, except invited speakers, must submit a summary of the findings they want to present. If the findings seem sufficiently interesting and believable to the reviewers—who are usually other scientists in the same field—the scientist will be allowed to present. Conferences give scientists the opportunity to network with colleagues at other institutions, potentially helping them set up new cross-institutional collaborations, and to get feedback that helps them prepare their work for publication in a peer-reviewed journal.

When a scientist submits a paper to a journal for publication, the journal's editor usually sends it to three independent reviewers who make comments, ask questions, and express their concerns. The reviewers may request that the scientist do more experiments, and/or challenge the scientist's interpretation of the results. The scientist can address the concerns of the reviewers and then resubmit the paper to the journal, unless the journal completely rejects the paper because of real or purported flaws in the science, or because the editor does not believe the paper fits with the theme of that particular scientific journal. There can be several phases of editing and review before a paper is published, and some papers will never make it to publication if the scientist cannot adequately respond to the concerns of the reviewers. The review process serves as quality control to prevent the publication of unsubstantiated claims. However, like any quality control process, it sometimes rejects outstanding work, and sometimes permits shoddy work to get through. As discussed later in the chapter, papers that are simply "before their time" may be rejected by the journal or, even if published, ignored by the scientific community. On the other hand, papers containing fraudulent data may make it past the reviewers and be published.

These flaws, while serious, need to be kept in perspective. In particular, they are not arguments against the importance of the scientific review process. A scientist's attempt to bypass peer review by pitching a claim directly to the media is a serious warning sign of possible intellectual dishonesty. If a discovery is exciting and the data are sound, the research should merit publication in a major scientific journal. It may get published in *Science, Nature*, or another journal that prints articles from all fields of science, or it may get published in one of the field-specific journals, such as *Cell*, the *Journal of the American Chemical Society*, or the *British Medical Journal*. Either way, the published article will include a detailed description of the procedure that the researchers followed to collect the data. In contrast, when reporters from the mainstream media or popular science journals write about discoveries for the general public, they tend to skim over the details about the methods used by the researchers. Popular accounts of scientific discovery are therefore considerably more palatable than research articles in scientific journals, but they do not contain adequate information for other scientists working in the field. Without detailed information about experimental procedures, other researchers are unable to determine whether there could be an alternative explanation for the results. They also cannot replicate the results. Ultimately, it is the replication of results by other researchers that is the test of the results' validity. Publication is not the final stage of the scientific process because when the review process fails to keep bunk from being published, future research sheds light on the error.

Arguably the most infamous example of results that were pitched directly to the media, only to turn out to be spurious, is the case of cold fusion. In the spring of 1989, Stanley Pons and Martin Fleischmann held a news conference to make the stunning announcement that they had managed to fuse atoms of deuterium at room temperature without using expensive equipment. Nuclear fusion provides the energy that powers the sun, and achieving nuclear fusion on Earth at low temperatures would be a major achievement. It would permit unlimited amounts of energy to be produced cheaply. Not surprisingly the cold fusion announcement created a hubbub within the scientific community and among the general public. The month after the announcement by Pons and Fleischmann, the American Chemical Society organized a symposium on cold fusion at its national conference. The symposium attracted 7,000 people, not a large number for a rock concert, but a huge draw for a set of talks about science. Two decades later, we do not have any cold fusion devices powering our homes or cars, nor are any on the horizon, although a small band of researchers is still working on the topic. The majority of researchers have written off cold fusion as a mistake, or outright fraud. Because Pons and Fleischmann announced their cold

fusion results to the media without publishing them in a scientific jour
nal, and they were secretive about their methods, it took time for other
researchers to come to the conclusion that the signs of fusion Pons and
Fleischmann claim to have seen were the result of experimental errors.
Had their results been subjected to peer review before their announcement to the media, these errors would very likely have been identified
before cold fusion fever spread worldwide.

In general, there is nothing wrong with scientists talking to reporters
about their research. Many scientists want to teach the public about their
work to inspire young people to study science and to convince taxpayers
of its value. Some public funding agencies, such as the U.S. National Science Foundation, even mandate that the scientists who receive funding
from them engage in activities to inform the public about their research.
The problem only arises when scientists promote their research to the
media in lieu of publishing it in a scientific journal, or when they make
claims that go far beyond those that are supported by existing scientific
research. Some scientific journals even have rules prohibiting scientists
from talking to the media until right before the scientist's paper is going
to be published by the journal. These rules are referred to as the
embargo policy. The purpose of the embargo is to avoid a cold fusion-
like scenario by making sure a research paper is available for critique by
other scientists when the popular press is reporting on the story. Therefore, claims should be interpreted with extreme caution if they have
been made directly to the media, especially if other scientists are greet-
ing them with skepticism.

Myth #5

The publication of findings is the endpoint of the scientific process.

No. In some ways, publication is the beginning because it allows
other scientists to build on the work. It also exposes the work to the
scrutiny of any scientist around the world.

Implications for making sense of scientific issues:

In considering the veracity of scientific findings, studies published
in a scientific journal should be given infinitely more weight than
those that are not, but beyond that, time is the most critical test.

The age of an idea is not proof of its accuracy, but ultimately time for further research is needed to confirm or disconfirm findings. A finding should be given more weight if there are multiple confirming instances, if the confirming instances were observed under many different conditions, and if some of the findings have disconfirmed alternative hypotheses. Also, a hypothesis is considered much stronger if it successfully predicts future observations, rather than merely accounting for existing observations.

The scientific review process is not flawless

The many levels of critique give the scientific process its strength, but no process is perfect. Sometimes good science does not get published, and sometimes bad science does.

Revolutionary ideas are sometimes overlooked

Barbara McClintock's research on "jumping genes," or **transposons**—bits of DNA that can move from one place on a chromosome to another—is an example of important science that initially failed to garner the attention it deserved. McClintock had collected reams of data to support her claims about transposons. She had meticulously documented how color changes in the kernels of the corn plants she bred could be linked to the changes in the chromosomes of those plants as seen through a microscope. She knew that her findings would come as a surprise to her fellow biologists, so before making them public, she spent six years collecting data to refute the objections to her findings that she anticipated other researchers would have. However, the field of genetics had not yet advanced to the point where it could provide a real mechanism for McClintock's observations.

It took more than 20 years from the time she made her research on transposons public to its recognition by the greater scientific community. This lack of acceptance could not be attributed to the marginalization of McClintock; she was already well known for her work on the genetics of corn. Also, some other corn geneticists did recognize the importance her work, and a few even had similar findings. The problem was that in the early 1950s, when McClintock first made her work public, biologists took for granted that genes were stable. It seemed unfathomable to think that genes could jump around on a chromosome—just as scientists did not initially believe that the continents could be moving.

New data and an explanatory mechanism led other scientists to accept that transposons were real and to recognize their significance. In the decades between the initial announcement of her findings and the research community's acknowledgement of their importance—ultimately earning her a Nobel prize—other research, including Watson and Crick's determination of the structure of DNA, and independent confirmation in bacteria of the sort of gene rearrangements McClintock had discovered, led to a sea change in the way scientists think about genetics. They stopped viewing genes as simply beads on a string—a chromosome—and in the face of volumes of data collected by independent researchers working on different problems, the notion that genes can move around came to be accepted.

The many historical examples of the scientific community ignoring ideas that are before their time, like those of Wegener and McClintock, are often exploited by cranks to argue in favor of their implausible schemes. Their arguments run as follows:

The scientific community is not accepting my revolutionary idea about _____ (insert topic) just as _____ (name of a famous scientist) was ignored by his/her contemporaries. Time will vindicate me, just as _____ (famous scientist) was vindicated. In the meantime, you can benefit from buying my _____ (name of product or book).

The problem with this argument is that while a number of scientists have been ignored and later vindicated, these examples are still relatively rare compared to all of the examples of individuals who put forth crazy ideas that have not been vindicated. The earth is flat. The earth is hollow. Maggots are spontaneously generated by rotting meat, and mice are spontaneously generated by linens sprinkled with a few grains of wheat. The bumps on people's skulls provide insight into their personalities and capabilities. Christ was an astronaut who traveled back in time in a yet-to-be-developed NASA time machine. The likelihood that the ideas of self proclaimed revolutionaries will end up on the crazy idea junk heap—along with flat Earth, hollow Earth, spontaneous generation, phrenology, and deity in a spaceship, respectively—is much greater than the likelihood that their ideas will revolutionize science. For that reason, the claim that revolutionary ideas are sometimes overlooked, while true, is a poor argument for the legitimacy of an idea. /

Myth #6

Many important ideas have been ignored in the past, so if someone claims to have ideas that are being ignored by the scientific establishment, there is a good chance that their ideas are correct.

No. For every outlandish-sounding idea that is later vindicated, hundreds of others will never be anything but bunk.

Implications for making sense of scientific issues:

As the famous astronomer Carl Sagan said, "Extraordinary claims require extraordinary evidence." Any purported discovery that overturns well-accepted theories of how the world works should be greeted with healthy skepticism, especially if it is based on anecdotal evidence and the discoverer is not even an expert in the field. Unpublished findings are not a good basis for making important decisions. Despite the problems with the scientific review process sometimes missing hot science and sometimes letting fraudulent science through, it is still the best mechanism that exists for evaluating the validity of claims. The scientific community is diverse, and it is highly improbable that the entire community would or could conspire against an individual. Alfred Wegener and Barbara McClintock knew that their colleagues would view their respective ideas about moving continents and jumping genes with skepticism. Neither claimed that the scientific community was conspiring against them because of it. In fact, they were both just as troubled as the rest of the scientific community by the lack of a plausible mechanism to explain their findings.

Fraud sometimes occurs

In addition to sometimes turning a blind eye on revolutionary ideas, reviewers and the rest of the scientific community can get tricked into believing bogus results. In 2002, scandal rocked the world of physics. Starting in the late 1990s, Jan Hendrik Schön, a young physicist from

Germany working at the world famous Bell Laboratories in New Jersey, and his colleagues there, published a string of papers that promised to revolutionize several fields. Just before the investigations into their work brought everything crashing down, the group was publishing at the remarkable rate of one paper every eight days, mostly in major journals. The researchers had been working on tiny electrical switches similar to the ones used in computers. They developed switches from a variety of materials and discovered that the switches had surprising properties. For example, by adding a very thin coating of the chemical aluminum oxide to the switches, they could get materials that were usually poor at conducting electricity to conduct it very well. This may not sound particularly exciting, but Schön's papers were among the most cited papers in physics, and had scandal not erupted, his work would have very likely earned him a Nobel Prize.

But on May 10, 2002, officials at Bell Labs launched an investigation of Schön's work after outside researchers noticed what appeared to be a duplication of data in multiple papers. Even before the discovery of duplicated data in Schön's papers, scientists were starting to raise questions about why other labs were not able to replicate many of Schön's amazing results, despite their efforts and the tens of millions of dollars being spent on research in the area. On September 25, 2002, a Bell Labs report concluded that Schön had committed widespread misconduct.

A few years after the scandal over Schön's research, Woo Suk Hwang, a South Korean researcher who published pioneering work on producing patient-specific stem cell lines, was found guilty of fabricating data. Again, the problems with the work were revealed when other scientists scrutinized it and attempted to replicate it after its publication. When scientists want to pursue a particular line of work, they check their materials, equipment, and procedures by comparing their results to the published results from an identical experiment by another scientist. If time passes and other researchers cannot get the experiments to work, the original research will fall under scrutiny. Both Schön and Hwang were on the cutting edge of very hot fields. They should have known that they would eventually be found out. Had they been working on some obscure problem, it may have taken much longer for their work to have been exposed as fraudulent. On the other hand, they would not have had the excitement of making headlines on a regular basis. We will probably never know why they acted unethically, but in the end, their careers were ruined. In an unprecedented move, the institution from which Schön earned his doctorate revoked his Ph.D., although there was no evidence he had fabricated any of that research.

Although these are examples of pathological science, in the end, time and scrutiny by the scientific community did get science back on course again. McClintock's story shows that time and the accumulation of evidence can vindicate the work of the maverick. Schön's and Hwang's stories show that it can also expose the charlatan. The examples of McClintock's, Schön's, and Hwang's work reveal what Evelyn Fox Keller, in her biography of Barbara McClintock, A *Feeling for the Organism*, referred to as the "tangled web of individual and group dynamics" that defines the growth of scientific knowledge. Indeed, individuals cannot push scientific knowledge forward alone; it is through multiple levels of interactions between the individual and the group that science advances.

As Harry learned from the Half-Blood Prince's potions book, there is a lot more to doing science than following a recipe. This chapter took that lesson further by laying bare the inner workings of the scientific process. However, Harry, Ron, and Hermione also learned that making potions was one thing, using potions on their adventures was another. Their adventures exploited Felix Felicis and Polyjuice Potion the way people who hold stake in an issue exploit scientific results for their own purposes. The production of scientific results is just the beginning of the plot. The adventure continues after the results are made public. The subsequent chapters of this book explore the twists and turns of plot that occur once scientific results make it into the public realm.

2

Who's who?: identify those who hold stake in an issue and what their positions are

The Web site DHMO.org (www.dhmo.org) is dedicated to raising the alarm about a colorless, odorless chemical that is widespread in the environment. According to the Web site, the chemical, dihydrogen monoxide (DHMO), has the following dangers:

- *Death due to accidental inhalation of DHMO, even in small quantities.*
- *Prolonged exposure to solid DHMO causes severe tissue damage.*
- *Excessive ingestion produces a number of unpleasant though not typically life-threatening side effects.*
- *DHMO is a major component of acid rain.*
- *Gaseous DHMO can cause severe burns.*
- *Contributes to soil erosion.*
- *Leads to corrosion and oxidation of many metals.*
- *Contamination of electrical systems often causes short-circuits.*
- *Exposure decreases effectiveness of automobile brakes.*
- *Found in biopsies of pre-cancerous tumors and lesions.*
- *Often associated with killer cyclones in the U.S. Midwest and elsewhere.*
- *Thermal variations in DHMO are a suspected contributor to the El Niño weather effect.*

—Dr. Tom Way, Director of Research for DHMO.org, Associate Professor of Computing Sciences at Villanova University

The site goes on to claim that DHMO is used in the production of biological and chemical weapons and pesticides, as a performance enhancer by elite athletes, and that it is even added to baby food and beverages that claim to be "all-natural." The folks at DHMO.org clearly want you to be outraged when you read about this widespread, insidious chemical, but hopefully you are at least a little skeptical, or are amused because you have figured out the punch line.

A closer look at the chemical formula of dihydrogen monoxide gives away the joke. Dihydrogen means two hydrogens. Monoxide means one oxygen. So our dangerous chemical is none other than H_2O, or water. The claims DHMO.org makes about the dangers of water are absolutely true. Yet these true claims are misleading. The reader is misled because certain information was provided while other information was withheld. For example, the gaseous form of water can cause severe burns, not because water is a dangerous, corrosive chemical, but rather because steam is hot.

The DHMO site is a clever joke, but it illustrates the theme of this chapter: Individuals or groups with a vested interest in convincing others of their point of view can be skillful at spinning information. Stakeholders may want us to buy certain products, make certain political decisions, or lead our lives in particular ways. This chapter provides an introduction to the different categories of individuals and groups that typically hold stake in scientific issues, and presents some tantalizing examples of the ways different stakeholders can inadvertently or deliberately distort information to present their viewpoints in the most favorable light.

People, positions, purposes

There is no single unbiased source of information that provides an accurate list of the pros and cons of making a particular decision. In general, each information source is biased to some degree, some sources much more than others. Although not all stakeholders deliberately try to mislead people, individual stakeholders' unique viewpoints lead each stakeholder to rank the importance of individual tradeoffs differently. As a result, a stakeholder may fail to mention a pro or con that someone else would consider critical, or may emphasize a pro or con that, given a more appropriate context for comparison, would not even exist. The first defense against being misled is to identify who is speaking, and what they have to gain or lose from the issue. Furthermore, there are categories of stakeholders whose voices should be considered, and sought out if necessary, when making decisions. To get a feel for the range of possible individuals and groups that hold stake in an issue, consider the mad cow disease controversy.

Mad cow disease—**bovine spongiform encephalopathy (BSE)**—is a disease that leads to severe degeneration of nerve cells. Brains of infected cows end up full of holes (spongy-looking, hence the name "spongiform"), and the animals become uncoordinated and eventually unable to stand. The disease was first recognized in 1986 in Britain, and scientists soon realized that feeding cows protein and mineral supplements derived from the carcasses of other cows spread the disease. The British authorities initially assumed that BSE could not be transmitted to humans. They based this assumption on the observation that a similar disease in sheep, which has been around for hundreds of years, has not spread to humans. But by 1996, a link was made between BSE and a new human neurodegenerative disease, dubbed **variant Creutzfeltd-Jakob Disease (vCJD)**. It is also now thought that BSE may have originated through the feeding of recycled sheep parts to cows.

In response to the BSE epidemic, hundreds of thousands cows in Britain were slaughtered and incinerated. Governments around the world banned the importation of British cattle and meat products, and banned the feeding of recycled cow protein and bone meal to cows. The United States began testing a small percentage of American cattle for BSE in 1990. British cattle that had been imported prior to the bans were tracked down, seized, and slaughtered. In 1999, the U.S. Food and Drug Administration (FDA) banned blood donations from people who had spent six months or more in Britain. These blood bans were later made more stringent and, as BSE was detected in several more European countries, extended to people who had lived in continental Europe.

After the discovery of vCJD, authorities in continental Europe and elsewhere reassured their citizens that BSE was a British problem. Having lived in France between 1996 and 1998, I experienced firsthand the efforts of the French authorities to convince the French public that the mad cow problem was localized to the other side of the English Channel. In the supermarket, packages of French beef were marked with "VF" stickers to reassure consumers that the meat was French—"viande française" (not "vache folle"—mad cow— as some consumers noted sarcastically). Meanwhile, British consumers reacted with outrage to the banning of the sale of beef on the bone and certain internal organs, which were considered more risky for transmitting the disease than muscle tissue.

American consumers did not pay much attention to mad cow disease until Oprah Winfrey weighed in on it. In 1996, Oprah interviewed a former cattle rancher turned vegetarian on her television show. After he talked about BSE and explained the practice of recycling protein and bone meal from cow carcasses to feed to cows, Oprah exclaimed, "This has stopped me cold from eating another burger." The next day, beef sales plunged to an all-time low, and the cattle ranchers responded by suing Oprah. The suit was later dropped. The ranchers also launched bumper stickers exclaiming, "The only mad cow in America is Oprah." The dip in beef sales was not long-lasting, and even after the first case of BSE was discovered in the United States in 2003, American consumers only briefly lost their appetite for beef.

Several of the major stakeholders in the BSE controversy should be apparent from this introduction. Cattle ranchers obviously have a lot to lose if consumers become wary of the beef supply, hence their outrage at Oprah. Similarly, the rendering industry—the industry that recycles animal carcasses into bone meal and protein supplements for livestock—does not want to fall victim to consumer outrage and government regulations. Pigs and chickens can still be fed these supplements, even though many have argued that the assumption a BSE-like disease could not arise in these animals is unjustified.

The stake of politicians and regulatory agencies in the BSE issue is complex. These groups need to keep consumers safe, but they also need to consider the economic consequences of imposing new regulations. For example, following the discovery of mad cow disease in the United States, many countries banned the importation of U.S. beef. Such decisions have far-reaching impacts. Declines in beef exports affect ranchers, the meat packing industry and manufacturers, retailers of processed food that contains beef, shipping companies, and other businesses that provide services to beef producers and processors. The government is under pressure to minimize these economic impacts by convincing other governments that the U.S. beef supply is safe, so exports can continue. Of course, minimizing economic impacts and ensuring consumer safety can be at odds.

The response of the U.S. Department of Agriculture (USDA) reflects the influence of these competing forces. On the one hand, the USDA increased the number of cattle that are tested for BSE each year. On the other hand, when Kansas-based Creekstone Farms wanted to do its own testing for BSE on all the cattle it slaughtered, to maintain its exports to Japan, which mandated such testing, the USDA refused permission. It cited concerns about Creekstone establishing a precedent that would force all meatpackers to test their cattle, which the USDA considered expensive and unnecessary.

No one is going to protest in favor of BSE, of course, but some stakeholders have something to gain from the concern over BSE. For example, organic farmers, who are prohibited from using animal-derived feed, can sell more beef to consumers worried about the safety of the conventional beef supply. Makers of kits to test cows for BSE are selling more of their products. Environmentalists promoting sustainable agriculture and lifestyles also see concern over BSE as an opportunity to emphasize other downsides of consuming a diet high in meat, in the hopes that the BSE controversy might make people more receptive to these arguments.

Seek out the voices of stakeholders in all categories and unearth the silent voices

Clearly, the controversy over mad cow disease involves a diverse set of stakeholders. In general, a wide variety of individuals hold stake in any science-related issue. The stakeholders for BSE, genetically engineered food (which is discussed in Chapter 3, "Decisions, Decisions"), global warming (covered in Chapter 5, "What Happens If...?"), and approval of a new drug to treat depression (see Chapter 8, "Society's Say") are listed in Table 2.1 and can be divided into several broad categories. The categories are based on who may gain or lose money, who makes the rules, who is indirectly affected in unforeseen ways, and other voices including advocates with nonfinancial interests, scientists, and reporters.

The groups listed in Table 2.1 are not completely homogeneous, and they do overlap. For example, individual scientists may have conflicting views on a controversy, and individual businesses within an industry may differ on what regulations they find acceptable. In addition, environmentalists may be business owners; individuals in all the other categories are also consumers; businesses and regulatory agencies employ scientists;

and there are many different types of media representing a wide variety
of perspectives; and so forth. Despite their overlap and heterogeneity,
familiarity with these different categories of stakeholders makes it easier
to elucidate the various stakeholders' voices when you are confronted
with a new controversy.

Table 2.1   Categories of stakeholders

	BSE	**Genetically engineered food**	**Global warming**	**Approval of a new drug for depression**
Who is purchasing or selling a product (involved in the controversy)?	Consumers	Consumers	Consumers	Patients
	Cattle ranchers	Conventional farmers	Fossil fuel-based energy producers	Pharmaceutical companies
	Meat packers/ processors	Manufacturers of processed food	Industries that burn fossil fuels (all, directly or indirectly)	Retail pharmacies
	Rendering industry			Health plans
	Supermarkets/ retail vendors	Supermarkets/ retail vendors	Vehicle manufacturers	
	Manufacturers of BSE test kits			
Who are competitors of the vendors?	Organic ranchers	Organic farmers	Renewable energy producers (wind, solar, geothermal)	Pharmaceutical companies that manufacture competing drugs.
	Those who sell alternatives to beef (other meat, Soya)	Those who sell non-genetically engineered specialty processed food	Nuclear power producers	Those who offer offer alternative (non-drug) treatments for depression
			Manufacturers of alternative (e.g., hydrogen-powered) vehicles	

	BSE	Genetically engineered food	Global warming	Approval of a new drug for depression
Who makes the rules?	Regulatory agencies (USDA, FDA)	Regulatory agencies (USDA, FDA, EPA)	EPA Politicians	FDA Politicians
	Politicians (in your country)	Politicians	Governments of other countries	Governments of other countries
	Governments of other countries	Governments of other countries	International agreements (e.g., Kyoto Protocol)	
	The WTO	The WTO		
Who gets caught in the crossfire?	Patients who need blood Potential blood donors	Citizens in developing nations (e.g., when governments refuse food aid because the food is genetically engineered)	Developing nations (subjected to environmental pressures America did not have during its development)	Patients (may end up on a drug due to high-pressure sales tactics, when another drug or treatment would have been more appropriate)
Others	Scientists Environmentalists The media	Scientists Environmentalists The media	Scientists Environmentalists The media	Scientists Doctors The media

Abbreviations: USDA: U.S. Department of Agriculture; EPA: Environmental Protection Agency; FDA: Food and Drug Administration; WTO: World Trade Organization.

Imagine that you had the opportunity to interview stakeholders in each category about their points of view on an issue and their rationales for their positions. If you started off with a black-and-white viewpoint, it would be difficult to maintain after these discussions because each stakeholder would introduce nuances. For example, the blood donation bans are a little-known and completely unexpected consequence of the practice of feeding rendered animal protein and bone meal back to cows. The bans introduce a unique set of questions and concerns to what initially appears to be controversy limited to farming practices. Similarly, the fact that the president of Zambia rejected a shipment of corn from the U.S. Agency for International Development because some of the corn was genetically modified introduces a whole new caveat of developed nations' attitudes toward these crops. Other African nations have also been reluctant to accept genetically engineered corn for fear that if some of it were planted, it could jeopardize future exports of any agricultural products to Europe, which has been hostile toward genetically engineered food.

Some viewpoints reach our ears more readily than others because certain stakeholders have characteristics that make them much more likely to get their voices heard. Obviously, financial resources make it easier for stakeholders to promote their messages. The old adage "money talks" is true. Money can be used to produce slick marketing campaigns. It can also be used to hire communications experts and writers who can help get a message to the media and encourage reporters to cover a company's latest developments. Marketing and communications are valuable strategies used by stakeholders with adequate resources, including corporations, unions, and other large special interest groups. As part of these efforts, groups may choose a charismatic leader who can serve as the public face to represent their interests, or the charismatic leader may by default become a leading voice for a cause. For example, former U.S. Vice President Al Gore has become a proponent of taking action to mitigate global climate change. Actor Christopher Reeve, after a spinal cord injury left him paralyzed and until his death, former First Lady Nancy Reagan, who lost her husband to Alzheimer's disease, and actor Michael J. Fox, who suffers from Parkinson's disease, all have promoted a stem cell research agenda. Their celebrity status gives the issues a human face and makes people listen to their viewpoints. In contrast, starving people in a drought-stricken region, children in impoverished inner-city schools, and other vulnerable members of society lack the resources to make their voices heard.

What issues are promoted and society's receptiveness to different individuals and messages can be arbitrary. Compelling images and powerful narratives get certain issues into the news, while other equally important issues languish. "Man bites dog" is a much more attention-grabbing headline than "dog bites man." Some issues, such as drought leading to starvation in Africa or humans dying from mad cow disease, become trendy for a while and are prominently covered by the media. Then public interest wanes, and reporters move on to other stories, making it seem as though the problem has disappeared, although suffering continues. The media itself is a stakeholder because newspapers and magazines want to increase their circulation; radio and television programs want to improve their ratings; and Web sites want to increase the traffic through them. As a result, the media often fails to present what we should hear, but instead, presents what they think we want to hear.

If one is passive about gathering information, it is not possible to develop an understanding of the range of issues and the positions of the various individuals and groups that hold stake in them. Seeking out the different stakeholders' perspectives elucidates the spectrum of tradeoffs of an issue and is necessary for balanced decision-making. Ideally, one would consult a variety of information sources using knowledge of the different categories of stakeholders to guide the search. The categories reveal what voices are missing from the mix, making it easier to seek them out, and/or make an educated guess about what the various positions may be. Since there are recurring themes and voices in different controversies, experience reasoning about one issue can be applied to new issues.

Ask yourself what motivates each stakeholder

Making balanced decisions about scientific issues would be relatively straightforward if it only entailed identifying the perspectives of the different stakeholders, coming up with a list of tradeoffs, and then deciding on the relative importance of the tradeoffs. However, to return to the idea that began this chapter, the information provided by a stakeholder may or may not be reliable. Stakeholders may unknowingly use inaccurate, incomplete, or outdated information, or they may deliberately spin data to bias their conclusions.

Determining how skeptical to be about information begins with identifying its source and what stake that individual or group has in convincing you of their point of view. For example, advertisements are low on the list of reliable information sources because their sole purpose is to sell a product. It is in advertisers' best interests to massage data to cast a product in the most favorable light. Many advertisements are disguised to appear informative or at least imply that the company advertising the product has your best interests at heart. Infomercials are an extreme example of this, as are those "paid advertisement" question and answer columns in magazines and newspapers. They may not lie outright for fear of litigation, but advertisers have an extensive bag of tricks to convince consumers of a product's merits, while downplaying its drawbacks. Stakeholders are not always trying to sell a product. Often, it is ideas that they want you to "buy." For example, if public interest groups want to acquire new members, they may emphasize possible hazards and sup-posed conspiracies to try to make people feel fearful or angry.

Each stakeholder's interest in convincing others of a point of view is not always blatantly obvious. Yet everyone is a stakeholder and filters information through a personal "lens." Stakeholders' motivations are diverse. In addition to money, stakeholders may be motivated by the need to save face, political pressures or pressures from an employer or other authority figure, ideology rooted in religion or social conscious-ness, or personal life circumstances, such as having a family member who suffers from a particular disease. The position adopted by an individual stakeholder may be fluid and dependent on external circumstances. For example, politicians sometimes get themselves in trouble by adopting different positions on gay marriage, abortion, stem cell research, and other ethically charged issues when they are speaking to a conservative audience than when they are speaking to a liberal audience.

Just because someone has a vested interest in influencing others does not mean that the person is lying. It is cynical to dismiss claims just because the individual making the claims has an interest in convincing others to adopt a particular point of view. An issue may indeed be impor-tant, but only someone with a strong enough stake in the issue is willing to spend the time and money needed to bring the issue to the attention of others. Just the same, it is important to be aware of the motivations of those trying to persuade others. Strong motivating factors are a reason to consider what stakeholders say with a healthy degree of skepticism. To verify the information they provide, try to trace stakeholders' claims and evidence back to their origins.

Remember the "broken telephone" effect and consult the original source

There is a children's game that illustrates how information can change more and more from its original meaning as it passes from one person to another. We called the game "Broken Telephone," and it was played by sitting in a circle and having one person whisper something to the next person, who passed it on to the next, and so on around the circle. The fun came in comparing what the last person heard to what the first person had originally said. Invariably, the original information was transformed into something very different. For instance, "My dog Sam likes Oreo cookies" might become "Monday I am learning cooking."

The science and health information that we get through the media or via word of mouth also passes through multiple sources before it reaches us. Often the information becomes distorted after it leaves the original source, or we only get part of the story and make incorrect assumptions based on what we hear. One example of a chain through which scientific information may pass is the following:

Scientific Paper => Press Release => Newspaper Article => Radio/Television Broadcast => **Radio Listeners or Television Viewers**

When a research paper is published in a scientific journal, the home institution of the paper's main author may translate the findings from the rather technical language used in scientific papers to a more palatable summary that is usually a page or two in length. The summary is referred to as a press release. It is passed along to reporters and is also made public on the Web, usually on the Web site of the author's home institution. If the science seems sufficiently interesting, a reporter may write an article about it for the newspaper. Another reporter from another newspaper, a magazine, or a radio or television station may see the newspaper article and decide to do a story based on that. At any of these steps, communication can break down and lead to distortions of information. Of course, good reporters try to trace information back to its source, but in this fast-paced world where information overload is common, that does not always happen.

One example where information has been distorted and then promulgated has to do with the Atkins diet. Many people believe the diet endorses eating a lot of meat and little else; however, even the most cursory look at an Atkins diet book or Web site makes it clear that this is false. The diet is more complex than the stereotype implies, particularly its emphasis on considering a food's glycemic index—impact on blood sugar—when making diet selections. In the case of the Atkins diet, the distortion of information may be caused by our inherent tendency to oversimplify. In other cases, the change in meaning from the original source reflects more nefarious intentions.

The rampant claims about indium (and other nutritional supplements) on the Internet are examples of deliberate distortions of information. **Indium** is a metal—element number 49 in the periodic table—that is used in the electronics industry. Indium does not have any known biological function, but according to some Web sites that sell indium supplements, it has the power to cure a large number of ailments, including fatigue, obesity, and cancer. Many of the Web sites present these claims without any supporting evidence, but the example of one claim, supported with reference to a specific scientific paper, clearly illustrates how stakeholders can distort evidence to suit their purposes. The claim is that indium can help people lose weight and is particularly effective for women. However, the scientific study cited had actually reported that indium stunted the growth of mice, especially female mice. The data in the scientific paper and the conclusions of its authors are very clear, and could not be inadvertently muddled into the claims that appeared on the Web site. Stunting the growth of mice is obviously not the same as helping women (or mice, for that matter) lose weight. Because other scientific studies have found that indium can cause liver and kidney damage, at least in high doses, this example clearly under-scores the need to consult the original source when making important decisions.

Just as with the broken telephone game, scientific information can be distorted in different ways depending on who are the intermediaries in the chain through which the information passes. Even when the links in the chain are supposed to be unbiased, different intermediaries can interpret identical information in different ways. Media reporting on sci-entific studies of the differences between men and women is a good example. Politically conservative and politically liberal papers put differ-ent spins on findings about male/female differences. In the August 2004 issue of the journal *Psychological Science*, psychologists Marianne LaFrance and Victoria Brescoll reported that newspapers with a politi-cally conservative editorial stance tended to report that gender differ-ences had a biological basis. In contrast, papers rated politically liberal, based on their editorial positions, were more likely to attribute the gen-der differences to environmental factors, such as social learning. How much nature (genes) and nurture (the environment) contribute to differ-ent personality traits is never clear-cut, and the psychologists did not find evidence that the newspaper reporters were deliberately falsifying data. The reporters were just automatically filtering the scientific findings through their own subjective views of the world. However, the psycholo-gists discovered that the reporters' slant had a profound effect on read-ers. After reading an article that suggested gender differences in an ability were due to social or cultural factors, readers were much more likely to say they believed people can change. After reading an article that suggested gender differences in ability were the result of biological factors, readers were more likely to say they believed that people cannot change.

Stakeholders have many ways of making their claims sound convincing. Because the route to any conclusion is not straightforward, it is not unusual for the opposing arguments of two stakeholders to both seem credible. After all, conclusions depend on the context in which tradeoffs are elucidated. Conclusions also depend on the validity of the evidence on which they are based. Stakeholders can fail to place information in an appropriate context. They can present pros and cons selectively, ignoring ideas that conflict with their position or just using different values when weighing tradeoffs. They can present evidence inappropriately or deceptively, for example by misinterpreting or manipulating statistics. Stakeholders can also use other tricks to persuade others. By appealing to attitudes and emotions, they often try to bypass the careful, logical thought processes that their listeners could use to find holes in their arguments. As you read the subsequent chapters, you will become increasingly resistant to the influence of stakeholders because the chapters reveal the potential pitfalls involved in making decisions about science-related issues. The next chapter delves into the colorful palette of possibilities that arise as one goes beyond the sound bites about scientific issues.

3

Decisions, decisions: elucidate all the pros and cons of a decision

We have the tendency to think of things in black and white. It's good or it's bad. You're with me or against me. It's all or nothing. Sound bites in the media and oversimplified perspectives presented by many other stakeholders often reinforce the idea that issues can be broken down into simple dichotomies. But in reality, whether science, politics, or personal relations, most issues have shades of gray and even brilliant splashes of color. Complexity and nuance are the norm, not the exception.

Even a seemingly simple decision such as choosing whether to go to a party has a list of pros and cons, or tradeoffs, associated with it. I might not get home until late, and I have an important meeting to go to in the morning. I might meet some interesting people. My ex-boyfriend might be there, and I don't want to see him. My friend might be mad if I don't go to her party. I'm really tired…. Making a decision involves reflecting on the pros and cons, ranking their importance, and maximizing the most important pros while minimizing the most important cons. In some situations, like the party example, one overriding pro or con may make the choice straightforward, and the careful consideration of options unnecessary.

The decision-making process is more challenging when dealing with complex issues where the pros and cons may be numerous, and some of the pros and cons may be hidden. Exactly what the choice is may not be obvious with many issues, although it may *seem* like there is an obvious choice. For example, a surgeon may make it appear that surgery is the only option by providing detailed information about knee surgery but completely failing to mention possible nonsurgical alternatives, such as orthopedic shoe inserts that correct alignment problems, exercise programs that strengthen the muscles supporting the joint, or new medications that reduce inflammation and promote healing. Likewise, a choice

43

may appear to be a dichotomy even if a middle ground exists. A choice may also be presented as the option of taking some action and not taking that action, without the recognition that maintaining the *status quo* is actually an alternative action with its own tradeoffs.

A decision is misguided unless the risks and benefits of all the relevant alternative actions are taken into consideration. Therefore, correctly identifying the available options and elucidating the pros and cons of each are the first steps toward making sound decisions about scientific issues. At first, exploring the nuances of a complex scientific issue feels like being immersed in the colors and dribbles of a Jackson Pollock painting. But an understanding of the kinds of nuances that arise and the themes of pros and cons that recur in different scientific issues can transform the unmanageable complexity into something much tidier. The result is still colorful and exciting, but more like the orderly, bright squares and stripes of Piet Mondrian than Pollock's chaotic splotches.

From black and white to vibrant technicolor

The importance of carefully analyzing choices is clearly illustrated by one excerpt from the ongoing controversy over genetically engineered food—food from plants with one or more genes added or modified via techniques of modern biotechnology. In May 1999, a study was published in the journal *Nature* that led to a plethora of media articles raising questions about the risks of genetically engineered plants. Environmentalists began dressing up as monarch butterflies in protest, and over time the monarch became a symbol of environmentalists' and others' concern, not solely about genetically engineered plants, but also about corporate control of agriculture and even globalization in general.

To put things into perspective, the *Nature* paper, written by three researchers from Cornell University, was just one page long and did not involve the study of monarch butterflies in the wild. The researchers took three-day-old monarch butterfly caterpillars from their laboratory colony and gave different groups of caterpillars one of three things to eat:

1. Plain milkweed leaves
2. Milkweed leaves dusted with corn pollen from nongenetically engineered corn
3. Milkweed leaves dusted with corn pollen from genetically engineered corn

Milkweed is what monarch caterpillars eat in the wild. Milkweed often grows within or near corn crops, so it is certainly possible for wild monarchs to encounter milkweed leaves sprinkled with corn pollen, including pollen from genetically engineered corn, which in 1999 made up around a quarter of the total corn crop in the United States. The genetically engineered corn contained a gene from bacteria for an insecticide, which protects the corn from the ravages of an insect pest known as the European corn borer. The insecticide is called **Bt** for the bacteria **Bacillus thuringiensis**, from which the gene was taken, and which produce the insecticide naturally. When a corn borer starts munching on Bt corn, the Bt reacts with certain chemicals naturally present in the insect's stomach, changing the Bt into a form that can punch holes in the stomach, thereby killing the insect. Our stomachs do not contain the chemicals necessary to convert Bt into its toxic form. Therefore, Bt is not harmful to us or other animals.

As illustrated in Figure 3.1, the Cornell researchers found that 100 percent of the butterfly caterpillars survived when they were fed plain milkweed leaves or milkweed leaves dusted with pollen from nongenetically engineered corn. However, only 56 percent of the caterpillars survived when they were fed milkweed leaves with pollen from corn containing the Bt gene. When the *Nature* paper was published, the eye-catching monarch butterfly became the poster child for the movement opposed to genetically engineered food, and the media began predicting that "Frankenfoods" would lead to the annihilation of these beautiful creatures.

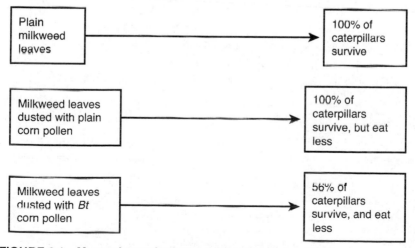

FIGURE 3.1   Monarch survival and milkweed consumption

Would the complete ban on genetically engineered food proposed by some be justified on the basis of this study?[1] With nearly half of the monarch caterpillars dying when exposed to *Bt* corn pollen in the lab, it is reasonable to conclude, as the authors of the study did, that we should carefully examine the environmental impact of *Bt* crops. However, there are two reasons why this study alone does not justify the indiscriminate banning of genetically engineered food. First, laboratory studies do not always replicate what goes on in the wild. Second, to grow or not grow genetically engineered food is an oversimplification and misrepresentation of the actual choice to be made.

The benefits and caveats of laboratory studies in general are discussed in Chapter 5, "What Happens If...?," and Chapter 6, "Specific or General," but it is useful at this point to highlight the specific caveats of the laboratory study reported in the *Nature* paper. In it, the monarch caterpillars were confined to small containers and had no choice about what food to eat. In the wild, the caterpillars could crawl to a different spot on a milkweed plant, perhaps to lower leaves, which might have less corn pollen. Interestingly, in the study, both groups of caterpillars that were fed milkweed leaves dusted with corn pollen ate less. One explanation for this is that caterpillars do not like corn pollen, even the corn pollen from nongenetically engineered plants. It is important to find out whether monarch caterpillars in the wild tend to avoid eating corn pollen. Recall that *Bt* is not toxic to insects unless they eat it. If the caterpillars do not usually eat corn pollen, then the introduction of *Bt* corn is unlikely to have the serious impact predicted by the laboratory study.

Furthermore, the paper did not provide any information about how much corn pollen is normally found on milkweed plants near corn crops. The researchers said that they dusted milkweed leaves with an amount of pollen "set to visually match densities on milkweed leaves collected from corn fields." However, the amount of pollen monarch caterpillars are exposed to in the wild would depend on wind and rain conditions, as well as whether the period of time when the corn is releasing pollen—which it does for less than two weeks—overlaps with the period of time between the hatching of monarch eggs and the caterpillars' metamorphosis into

[1] Note that since 1999 there have been multiple studies to investigate the effects of *Bt* crops on beneficial insects like monarch butterflies. Here I focus on the initial study that raised the alarm about these crops, because the media and public reaction to it was vocal and lacking in careful, rational, reflective analysis.

adults. Note that adult monarchs do not eat milkweed leaves; they drink nectar, and because nectar is found within flowers, adult monarchs are unlikely to consume *Bt*. In short, many variables in the wild were not replicated in the laboratory, and these variables would need to be investigated before drawing firm conclusions about the risks of *Bt* corn on monarchs.

Nuance is the norm

The authors of the *Nature* paper have themselves admitted that their study did not conclusively prove *Bt* corn is a danger to monarchs, but let us assume for the sake of argument that this could be concluded. Would that then justify the banning of genetically engineered food? In fact, the issue is still much more nuanced than it appears on the surface. In this example, it is possible to identify three levels of nuance, which, when overlooked, lead to the misidentification of the decision to be made. The first two levels of nuance have to do with recognizing that that the decision to ban genetically engineered food involves an overgeneralization about genetically engineered food on the basis of one crop. Other genetically engineered crops should be considered as well. The third level of nuance involves considering genetically engineered food in the larger context of agricultural practices.

The **first level of nuance** is that there are many different varieties of *Bt* corn, some of which do not produce *Bt* in the pollen. Which parts of the corn plant will produce *Bt* depends on where in the corn chromosomes the *Bt* gene inserts itself, a process that is fairly random. To protect against insect attack, the *Bt* needs to be produced in the parts of the plant that an insect would eat, stems, leaves, and so on, and there is no advantage to the farmer for the corn to produce insecticide in the pollen. There are varieties of *Bt* corn with negligible or no *Bt* in the pollen, and these should be as safe to monarchs as nongenetically engineered corn, since the pollen is the only part of the corn plant that travels any distance away from the boundaries of the crop. Switching to a variety of *Bt* corn that does not produce *Bt* in the pollen would protect monarchs without adverse effects to farmers. In fact, seed companies voluntarily stopped selling varieties of corn with high levels of *Bt* in pollen on the basis of the findings of the *Nature* paper and the subsequent public outcry. Therefore, *Bt* corn varieties must be compared to one another before conclusions are drawn.

The **second level of nuance** is that *Bt* corn is not the only genetically engineered crop, and even if the risks of *Bt* corn were found to outweigh its benefits, this would not justify the indiscriminate banning of all
genetically engineered crops. Each of the many types of genetically engineered crops has its own set of risks and benefits. For instance, unlike
plants designed to produce their own insecticide, there is no reason to
think that crops engineered to contain more nutrients would be dangerous to wildlife. Not only should nutrient-enhanced crops pose no threat
to wildlife, they could have important health benefits to humans. Treating genetically engineered crops as a monolithic evil ignores their potential for good. In other words, this level of nuance involves putting *Bt* corn
in the context of other genetically engineered crops.

The **third level of nuance** is that "to grow or not to grow" genetically engineered crops is not really the question. The true choice being
made is between genetically engineered crops and nongenetically engineered crops raised using any number of, often not benign, agricultural
practices. Once made explicit, this probably seems perfectly self-evident,
but restating the question in this way has profound implications for how
one judges the advantages and disadvantages of genetically engineered
crops. It does not appear that people automatically think of the issue in
these terms. This was clear in my own interviews and conversations
about the monarch study and other possible environmental implications
of genetically engineered crops with adolescents and adults, many of
whom were highly educated. People, even those with strong science
backgrounds, rarely pointed out that conventional—that is nonorganic,
nongenetically engineered—crops also have negative impacts on the
environment, and that these impacts need to be taken into consideration
when assessing the risks of genetically engineered crops. The popular
press also largely failed to put the findings of the *Nature* paper in the
context of other agricultural practices, even though in the final lines of
the paper, the authors argue that it is essential to gather the additional
data necessary to evaluate the risks of genetically engineered crops compared to the risks of pesticides and other methods of controlling pests.

The reality is that conventionally grown corn crops are sprayed with
pesticides 15 to 20 times during a growing season, a practice that cannot
be good for monarchs or other beneficial insects living near these crops.
(Note that *Bt* crops are also sprayed with pesticides because the *Bt* only

kills certain insect pests.) Organically grown crops may sound like an idyllic alternative to conventional or genetically engineered crops, but organic crops constitute a small percentage of all crops grown in the United States. Furthermore, contrary to popular belief, organic farmers do use pesticides; they just cannot use most man-made chemicals. Ironically, of the many chemicals approved for use on organic crops, Bt, in the form of a spray, has been widely used by organic farmers. It is improbable that Bt in the spray form would be any less likely to end up on milkweed plants bordering crops than the Bt in the pollen of genetically engineered corn.

Although some fear the actual procedure by which a gene is introduced into a crop plant to genetically engineer it, there is no evidence that this manipulation is any more risky than traditional forms of crop breeding. While traditional crop breeding—crossing plant varieties and selecting offspring with certain characteristics, often over many generations—has been used in the development of nearly every variety of crop plant grown today, it has also yielded some crops that were unexpectedly too dangerous to go to market. This includes potatoes that produced unacceptable levels of toxins and celery containing chemicals known as psoralins that caused the harvesters' arms to develop rashes.

A final complicating wrinkle is that some genetically engineered crops that have been criticized because of their potential risks to the environment have counterparts from traditional breeding with identical potential risks. An example is herbicide-resistant crops. These crops allow a farmer to spray certain herbicides to kill weeds without harming the crop plants. However, if these plants interbreed with nearby weeds, they could pass this resistance on to their offspring, leading to weeds that withstand the herbicide. Ultimately this may mean that farmers will have to turn to stronger herbicides that are more harmful to the environment. Since there exist both genetically engineered and traditionally bred herbicide-resistant crops, the potential risk of herbicide-resistant plants has nothing to do with the genetic engineering *per se*.

Determine the appropriate scope of the choice and compare to relevant alternatives

Talk about a rainbow of nuances! Concluding from the monarch butterfly laboratory study that genetically engineered food should be banned simplified a complex issue into a black-and-white choice, a choice that was misleading because it did not encompass all alternatives. Determining what the alternative options were required narrowing the scope of the choice to be made—that is, the study did not speak to all genetically engineered crops, or even all *Bt* corn, but rather one particular variety of *Bt* corn. Elucidating the options also required finding the appropriate big picture context for comparison—in other words, how this genetically engineered crop fared with respect to food grown using other agricultural practices. A series of questions about genetically engineered food, ranging from oversimplified to appropriately nuanced, is shown in Table 3.1.

TABLE 3.1   Refining choices

Black and white ➡			Technicolor
Should we ban genetically engineered food?	How safe is this specific variety of genetically engineered corn?	What are the risks and benefits of other genetically engineered crops?	How does a particular genetically engineered crop compare to its conventional or organic alternative?

Like with the controversy over genetically engineered food, when people argue for or against a particular technology, policy, course of action, and so on, it is common for them to lump all aspects of the innovation together and imply that the choice is simply one of adopting or not adopting it. Both proponents and opponents of its adoption frequently frame the choice in this oversimplified way. For example, some proponents of increased regulation of nanotechnology research and development have attempted to scare people with "grey goo" scenarios. Grey goo is the imagined consequence of self-replicating nanomachines that reproduce uncontrollably, such that everything becomes covered in them. The possibility of grey goo, some say, makes nanotechnology dangerous. On the other hand, opponents of new oversight of nanotechnology research point to the fact that nanotechnology is already being used without dire consequences. Therefore, they argue, new oversight is not necessary because the *status quo* is working. Both camps are using over-simplified reasoning. Just as the discussion of the genetically engineered food controversy made it clear that all genetically engineered crops cannot be lumped together, all nanotechnology cannot be lumped together. Nanotechnology is as varied as its larger "macrotechnology" counter-part—that is, the everyday objects with which we are all familiar, such as furniture, appliances, and vehicles. Many nanotechnologies may be perfectly safe, but that does not imply that all nanotechnologies are safe. On the other hand, even if self-replicating nanomachines could run amok and replicate into grey goo, that does not mean nanotechnology is dangerous in general. Scientists do not even know how to make nanomachines that reproduce. Grey goo is not a potential risk of currently available nanotechnologies, such as the tiny carbon nanotubes that reinforce golf clubs and baseball bats. However, there is evidence that nano-sized particles of certain shapes can be harmful to the lungs if they are inhaled. Therefore, each nanotechnology application must be considered individually and compared with the relevant alternatives, just as each unique genetically engineered crop needs to be considered in the context of alternative agricultural methods.

In the short term, this way of thinking about an issue may appear to complicate things, but in the long term it actually makes reasoning easier. This is because the more nuanced way of thinking about a controversy facilitates the integration of new information about it. For example, if you hear about a new genetically engineered nutrient-enhanced crop that may be able to save the lives of people in the developing world, you do not have to completely rethink your position on genetically engineered food. You could accept the merits of the new crop, while still holding onto your concerns about another crop. In other words, in the long run, the controversy will seem less confusing if you avoid taking a black-and-white view. People often become frustrated by discord on scientific issues because it seems that opposing viewpoints are hopelessly irreconcilable. As a result, it is easy to become cynical and disengaged and decide that it is not worth trying to make sense of scientific issues. Keeping in mind that both opponents and proponents often overgeneralize and ignore the appropriate context provides a critical starting point for reconciling opposing viewpoints, either by finding a middle ground, or by recasting the issue in a more appropriate way by comparing all the relevant options.

Finding the appropriate scope and context for comparison are just the first steps in making a sound decision about a technology or course of action. Not only do stakeholders overgeneralize and fail to compare alternative options, they also omit many important risks and benefits from their arguments. Because any decision has multiple risks and benefits, it is misleading to consider a risk or benefit in isolation from the other positive or negative consequences of making a decision. Risks and benefits need to be considered in the context of one another. To elucidate the tradeoffs, it is vital to have an understanding of the kinds of risks and benefits that recur commonly in science-related decisions. Familiarity with these themes makes it possible to make educated guesses about what hidden tradeoffs exist. Identifying themes of tradeoffs is the focus of the next section.

Say "yes" to one and leave the other behind

In their document outlining what science concepts and processes students should learn in school, the American Association for the Advancement of Science stressed the importance of being able to assess tradeoffs:

> *The concept of tradeoff in technology—and more broadly in all social systems—is so important that teachers should put it into as many problem-solving contexts as possible. Students should be explicit in their own proposals about what is being traded off for what. They should learn to expect the same of others who propose technical, economic, or political solutions to problems.*[2]

Not only do we need to recognize that decisions have tradeoffs, but we also need to know how to seek out information about what the tradeoffs are when those making the claims fail to provide that information. While this may seem daunting, decisions about a wide range of science-based issues involve similar themes of tradeoffs: the environment, human health, economics, and ethics. Knowledge of these themes and

---

[2] Material reprinted from *Benchmarks for Science Literacy* (1993) with permission from Project 2061, on behalf of the American Association for the Advancement of Science, Washington, DC.

how they play out in various issues can be applied when reasoning about new issues. Let us briefly consider some contemporary issues to gain a sense of the types of tradeoffs that arise.

Know the themes of risks and benefits that arise in science-related issues

Environment. The controversy over genetically engineered food involves a wide range of tradeoffs. The first part of this chapter revealed that environmental issues play an important role in the controversy. Crops that produce their own insecticides could harm beneficial insects. At the same time, such crops could reduce the need for sprayed pesticides. Crops engineered to resist an herbicide could cross with nearby weeds and lead to "superweeds" that resist the same herbicide, causing farmers to use more and stronger herbicides to deal with this new weed population. On the other hand, there is an environmental benefit of crops that resist herbicide. After spraying herbicide to kill weeds, farmers usually till their fields and leave them fallow to give the herbicide time to break down before planting crops. Tilling and leaving fields fallow results in erosion. With the herbicide-resistant crops, farmers can plant the crop, let it grow until it is firmly established and holding the soil in place, and then spray the crop with an herbicide that kills only the weeds. This method reduces erosion.

Human health. Issues of human health also arise in the genetically engineered food controversy. Nutrients can be added to food using genetic engineering. Research is ongoing to develop a variety of rice that contains sufficient beta-carotene—a compound that the body can convert into vitamin A—to help the millions of people suffering from vitamin A deficiency, especially those in countries where the majority of the caloric intake is from rice. Genetic engineering can also be used to remove toxins and allergens from food. This would be a significant breakthrough because food allergies afflict between 1 percent and 2 percent of the population. On the other hand, there is some concern that gene rearrangements caused by genetic engineering could inadvertently introduce new allergens into food.

Economics. Economics is the final broad theme in the genetically engineered food controversy. Economics comes into play at a global scale, with international trade, and at the scale of individual farmers and consumers. Some countries have refused to import genetically

engineered food, or have demanded labeling schemes that food manufacturers consider too expensive and impractical. Nevertheless, farmers
were quick to adopt certain genetically engineered crops, especially herbicide-resistant soybeans and insecticide-producing cotton, to increase
yields and profits. Proponents of genetically engineered crops have predicted that consumers would also see benefits in the form of lower prices
at the grocery store. On the other hand, opponents worry about the profits being reaped by the large biotechnology companies that sell genetically engineered seeds, and corporate control of agriculture.

Ethics. Environment, human health, and economics are the three
main themes of tradeoffs in the controversy over genetically engineered
food. A fourth theme, ethics, also arises, but most people are not very
concerned about the ethics of changing genes in plants because humans
have been manipulating plants for thousands of years. For example, corn
is a descendent of a grasslike plant called teosinte, which has very small
cobs and unpalatably hard kernels. It is thought that between 5,000 and
7,000 years ago, Central American farmers developed corn over a century or more of growing and selecting teosinte with fewer branches and
larger cobs. Modern breeding programs, which predate the introduction
of genetic engineering, further transformed corn into the familiar tall,
straight plant with enormous cobs and kernels. Genetic engineering is
the latest tool in a long history of plant breeding. Therefore, while
genetic engineering may introduce some unique environmental and
human health risks and benefits, the objection that we simply should not
alter plants is moot.

We all know ethics plays a role in science controversies, and it does
(vociferously) in the controversy over the use of embryonic stem cells. In
fact, the ethical objections over the source of the stem cells has often
overshadowed other tradeoffs in the controversy. For instance, could
stem cell treatments be made relatively safe for patients or would the
risk of injected cells rapidly proliferating and becoming cancerous always
exist? If these treatments could be made to work well, would this extend
people's life spans? Doing so comes with economic tradeoffs. Would we
have to reform social security or push back the age of retirement? There
are even indirect environmental effects if people end up living longer,
since—assuming constant birth rate—we would have more people
around consuming more of the earth's resources. These potential pros
and cons should be brought to the fore despite the highly polarized
debate over ethical issues.

In the many issues that we tend to classify as environmental, including global warming, declines in biodiversity, and air and water pollution, economics is often pitted against preserving the environment. However, these issues also directly or indirectly impact human health and well-being. For example, climate change can alter the distribution of mosquitoes that carry diseases such as malaria, bringing the disease, now mostly confined to the tropics and subtropics, to more temperate regions of the world. Environmental issues also usually have an ethical component because they often cause the greatest harm to the poorest people.

On its surface, the bovine spongiform encephalopathy (BSE) or mad cow disease controversy introduced in Chapter 2, "Who's Who?," exemplifies a tradeoff between economics and human health. Farmers fed cows protein supplements made from rendered cow carcasses because it was a cheap source of protein. Unfortunately, this practice ended up spreading a neurodegenerative disease among cows, and the disease ultimately spread to humans. The decision not to require BSE testing on every cow slaughtered for human consumption also trades off profit versus human health. Environmental issues are less obvious, but play an important role in this controversy. Replacing the protein in cows' diets would require the growing of additional crops, which could push agriculture into areas that used to be wild. This translates to habitat loss and potential decreases in biodiversity. Disposing of all the cow carcasses that used to be recycled would also use up land or require incineration, which creates air pollution.

These three themes of tradeoffs—environment, human health (well-being/comfort), and economics—recur in many different controversies. Of course, not all decisions involve tradeoffs in all three themes. In a medical decision, the environment and economics—assuming you have good health coverage—may not play a role. It could be a matter of trading off risks and benefits within the theme of human health. For example, the most effective treatment for a particular ailment could have the risk of long-term side effects. Other treatments may not work quite as well in the short term, but could be safer in the long term.

Long-term versus short-term. Immediate versus enduring risks and benefits is an important subtheme to consider in evaluating tradeoffs. Under each theme of tradeoff, it is possible to further classify each risk or benefit as something that will happen immediately or in the near future, or something that may not happen for a long time, even many

years after the decision was made. For example, because they reduce tilling, herbicide-resistant crops have environmental benefits in the first
year or few years that they are being grown. After multiple years of growing the same crop and using the same herbicide, the emergence of herbicide-resistant weeds can necessitate the use of chemicals that are more
harmful to the environment. Another example is that logging projects
may be considered beneficial by some native people in South and Central America because they create jobs and income in the short term.
However, in the long term, sustainable harvesting of nuts, medicinal
plants, and other forest products could actually lead to greater economic
gain.

It is human nature to focus on short-term gain and ignore long-term
consequences. Many of the environmental problems facing us, including
pollution, global climate change, loss of biodiversity, and water short-
ages, result from people's tendency to value immediate benefits over
detrimental effects that only become obvious down the road. Part of the
reason for people's tendency to focus on the short term is that the individuals getting the short-term benefits are often not the same ones suffering from the long-term consequences. However, selfishness cannot
entirely explain this tendency. When it comes to our own lifestyle choices
and medical decisions, we still tend to focus on the short term to the
detriment of the long term. Therefore, it is essential to make a conscious
effort to assess the possible long-term risks when making decisions.

Assessing long-term risks and benefits is inherently more difficult
than assessing short-term risks and benefits. Usually there is considerably more uncertainty about what will happen in the long term. One
cause of the uncertainty is that technologies have the potential to be used
in unforeseen ways. For example, chemical fertilizer has helped dramatically increase crop yields to feed a burgeoning population. However,
fertilizer can also be used to make explosives. It was used with devastating consequences in the 1995 bombing of the Oklahoma City Federal
Building. In contrast, many of the technologies developed primarily for
defense purposes, such as satellites, have been applied in countless
peaceful ways. Another reason for the uncertainty associated with long-
term risks and benefits is that it is difficult to predict how future conditions may change, and how those changes may interfere with predictions
about future consequences. For example, the accuracy of estimates of

global temperature increases based on emissions of man-made green-house gases depends on how natural climate variables will change in the coming years and decades. If the sun's output should decline, as it does periodically, this could offset the warming predicted to be caused by increases in carbon dioxide and other greenhouse gases.

Given the uncertainty involved in predicting long-term risks and benefits, it is tempting to ignore them. For instance, climate change skeptics argue that we should not take action to mitigate climate change unless we are absolutely certain that it is happening. However, most things in science are not completely certain. If we ignored everything except those few things of which we are certain beyond a shadow of a doubt, we would have a limited and unrealistic picture of the consequences of our decisions. Therefore, instead of ignoring the long-term implications, it is important to make every effort to determine what they could be, get a good estimate of their size or most likely range in size, and weigh them along with the other tradeoffs. The likelihood of a long-term risk or benefit can be taken into consideration during the weighing process, but, even if a risk or benefit is unlikely, it should not simply be ignored.

Just as themes of risks and benefits recur in different controversies, recurring themes of contexts can be used to identify and evaluate pros and cons. Some pros and cons require effort to uncover, and not every purported risk or benefit is as realistic or meaningful as claims may imply. The preceding discussion showed how comparing technologies (such as forms of agriculture) to each other could help reveal which risks and benefits were unique to a particular technology and which were common to alternative technologies. The comparison is important because if a risk or benefit is not unique to a new technology, then it is not a sufficient reason to endorse or demonize it. Comparing technologies to one another is just one of many ways to put things in context. The next chapter describes the many types of contexts that can be used to evaluate risks and benefits.

4

Compare and contrast: place alternatives in an appropriate context to evaluate tradeoffs

The major causes of concern are still with us. The number of people hospitalized after a trouser accident (up from 5137 to 5945) is worryingly high, while the drop in injuries inflicted by armchairs (down from 18,690 to 16,662) leaves little room for complacency. Hospitalizations from socks and tights have also risen (10,773 compared to 9843 previously), while injuries inflicted by vegetables remain unacceptably high at 13,132 compared with the previous year's 12,362. The number of accidents involving tree trunks has also risen from 1777 to 1810, while leaf accidents have soared from 664 to 1171....

—*New Scientist*, June 9, 2001

As shown by *New Scientist's* spoof of the Home and Leisure Accident Surveillance System report from Britain's Department of Trade and Industry, it is easy to get an unrealistic sense of the significance of risks (or benefits) in the absence of an appropriate context. Chapter 3, "Decisions, Decisions," showed how placing things in an appropriate context can reveal when an apparent choice does not really accurately represent the available options. This chapter explores how context makes it possible to assess the plausibility and significance of each claim or piece of evidence.

Context connections

A wide variety of types of contexts is useful for different issues. History
and geography can provide useful contexts. Also, several types of contexts can be used to make sense of numbers, which pepper the arguments of proponents and opponents of technologies, policies, and
procedures. Numbers can be misleading because their meaning changes
depending on how they are presented. Putting statistics in an appropriate context is just one aspect of critical thinking about statistics. Other
challenges of reasoning about statistics are addressed in Chapter 7, "Fun
Figures." Note that sometimes the media will use more eye-catching statistics in headlines and sound bites, but present the less-misleading figures lower down in the article or toward the middle or end of a news
broadcast. Paying attention to how the numbers are expressed can reveal
what they really mean. Putting things in context is not just a matter of
comparing one thing to another; it is also a matter of re-expressing ideas
in different ways to get a better grasp of their true meaning.

Compare technologies to other technologies

To come up with a balanced assessment of the genetically engineered
food controversy, it was important to compare one form of agriculture
(genetically engineered) to another (organic or conventional nonorganic)
without lumping all genetically engineered crops together. This is true
for any technology or procedure. To evaluate the merits of a particular
innovation, it should be compared to other innovations that serve a similar purpose, but all aspects of a particular innovation should not be
lumped together. For example, the risks and benefits of building a new
hydroelectric dam would need to be compared to the risks and benefits
of pursuing alternative sources of power, without lumping all forms of
renewable energy together. Expected outcomes of a surgical procedure
would need to be compared to those of other methods of treating a particular ailment, but without assuming that all surgical procedures would
compare to nonsurgical alternatives in the same way.

Put findings in a geographical context

It is easy to be insular and forget that people in different countries face
many similar problems. Some struggles are unique to particular nations,

but for the most part, it is possible and relevant to look to policies and technological solutions in other countries to see how they compare to those in one's own country. Also, in this global economy, it is often important to look outside one's borders to fully understand issues. For example, a study showing that manufacturing jobs are declining in the United States might lead to the conclusion that manufacturing jobs are moving to developing countries, where labor is cheaper. However, if there are worldwide declines in the numbers of manufacturing jobs, then a more suitable conclusion could be that increased mechanization is reducing the number of workers needed.

Consider the historical context

The cause of an observation or the relative importance of a policy can be exposed by comparing it to the relevant past situation. For example, correcting for inflation, it is possible to compare current spending on health care, education, the space program, defense, and so on to what was spent in the past to get a better sense of what the numbers mean. In the case of declining manufacturing jobs, putting declines into a historical context might reveal that these jobs were declining in the United States even before a controversial free trade agreement came into effect. If so, the agreement could not be responsible, or at least not entirely responsible, for the observed declines.

Express figures on a comprehensible scale

Statements about a nation's economy or the economic costs of specific policies usually contain huge numbers, billions or trillions of dollars. These numbers are so far outside the range of our everyday experience, that it is hard to fathom what they really mean. Even billionaires would have trouble envisioning how large a pile a billion dollar bills would make. After all, they hardly keep that kind of money lying around the house. Therefore, huge numbers must be placed into a context that enables people to make sense of them. One possibility is to express the figures as an amount per capita. In other words, how much would every man, woman, and child need to pay to cover the cost of the policy? Alternatively, the figures could be expressed in terms of a percentage of a nation's Gross Domestic Product, or as a percentage of the total tax dollars collected. Re-expressing economic data in this way can be useful for smaller numbers too. For example, housing costs around the country are more meaningful when they are considered in the context of the per capita income in each region. Expressing figures per capita or changing raw data (number of cases) into a percentage (of the population), or vice versa, can often change the conclusions you would draw from the numbers. If you heard that twice as many people contracted rabies this year as last year, you might be concerned that rabies was getting out of control. On the other hand, if you found out that last year only one person in the entire country contracted rabies, compared to two this year, then clearly there would be a lot less reason for concern. Similarly, an ailment that afflicts 3,000 to 4,000 people in the United States sounds a lot more common than one that afflicts one out of 100,000 people, but these are just different ways to express the same number.

Qualify the figures according to the circumstances under which they hold true

Some figures are relevant only to a portion of the population, or apply only under certain conditions. For example, when trying to ascertain the most dangerous sports, it is not sufficient to compare the numbers of people dying or being injured while engaging in different activities. If more people end up in the emergency room from playing Frisbee than from swinging on a trapeze, this obviously does not mean that playing Frisbee is inherently more dangerous than swinging on a trapeze. Many more people play Frisbee than swing on trapezes. Therefore, the figures must be expressed relative to the number of people involved in each activity. Risk needs to be translated into a percentage of the relevant population to provide a sense of the danger to any individual participating in that activity. In other words, it needs to be put in the context of the relevant population. This rule applies in many different situations, such as deciding what vehicle is safest, what medical procedure has the least risk, or what travel agency has the highest customer satisfaction.

Ask how the numbers being cited compare to "normal"

In 2001, a study of children beginning kindergarten showed that 17 percent of children who had spent 30 hours or more per week with someone other than their mother (for example, in day care) were rated aggressive, but only 6 percent of children who had stayed home with their mothers were rated aggressive. The news media reported these findings as meaning that children who attend day care learn to be unusually aggressive. However, putting the statistics in context reveals that the stay-at-home children were unusual. The study measured aggressiveness using a standardized test. Similar to an I.Q. test, when the aggressiveness test is administered to a large number of people, a bell curve of scores results. That is, the majority of scores cluster around the average, and smaller numbers of people get very high scores and very low scores. Subjects above a certain score on the test are rated aggressive, and it turns out that in any large, random population approximately 17 percent of test takers score high enough to be rated aggressive. What is more, as the stay-at-home children gained more experience interacting with other children in school, their scores became more similar to the scores of the general population. Anecdotal reports from day care workers also suggested that children who stayed at home were initially fearful and clung to their parents, rather than interacting with the other children. Clearly, the conclusions drawn from the 6 percent and 17 percent figures are very different when compared in the context of what is considered normal. A similar pitfall occurs when the number of people dying of cancer or having miscarriages after being exposed to some chemical is brandished about as proof that the chemical is dangerous. Such numbers are utterly meaningless unless they are compared to the number of people suffering similar problems, even though they have not been exposed to the chemical.

Be careful not to be misled by averages

Averages are a familiar way of expressing data. Most everyone has calculated the average of a set of figures by adding them up and dividing by the number of figures in the set. Although averages are seemingly straightforward, they can be misleading.

Put the average in context of the majority

An average seems like something that applies to everyone. That is the "baggage" associated with the term. Read that the average tax cut is $300, and it is tempting to think about fun things to do with that anticipated windfall. Learn that the average salary is $80,000 per year, and it is natural to think that is what an average Joe at the company earns. However, many different combinations of numbers can yield the same average. Therefore, the figure provided for the average tax cut may be very misleading. If a tax cut is based on a percentage of people's income, those with modest incomes will get much less than those in the highest income brackets. Likewise, the average salary can be misleading because it is often skewed by the salaries of the highest paid executives. That is, a few very large numbers in a list of figures can dramatically increase the average. Because of this effect, it may be more meaningful to express numbers in terms of a majority or median. For example, the average tax cut may be $300, but the majority of people may get a tax cut of less than $20. Similarly, the average income at company X may be $80,000, but the median income at Company X may be $55,000 per year (see Table 4.1). The median salary—the middle salary if salaries were listed from smallest to largest—is not skewed by the few high salaries at the top of the list.

Table 4.1   Salaries at company X

Office Assistant	$25,000
Production Line Worker 1	$35,000
Production Line Worker 2	$40,000
Production Line Worker 3	$44,000
Quality Control Assessor	$55,000
Sales Representative	$57,000
Machinist	$58,000
Production Manager	$96,000
President	$310,000
Median Salary	*$55,000*
Average Salary	$80,000

Consider the range of the data that were averaged

Since the average does not provide insight into what the raw data look like, another useful piece of information is the range—or **spread**—of data from which the average is calculated. The numbers can be tightly clustered together, or there can be some very high numbers and some very low numbers. In addition, even when the average has remained stable over time, the spread of data may have changed. For instance, average pay can hold steady, while the number of moderate paying jobs declines and the number of low and high wage jobs increases. Clearly, a change in low-, middle-, and high-paying jobs has potential economic repercussions, but the relevant information is hidden by the stability in the average. Considering the range is also useful when interpreting the results of medical tests, environmental tests, and similar types of analyses. It can be misleading to compare a test result on the level of a certain chemical in an individual's blood to the average of such test results in a population, or to compare the nutrient concentration in a particular lake to the average of test results on various bodies of water. If a test result is not exactly average, it does not say anything about the health of a person or ecosystem. In fact, there may be no single test result that has the exact same value as the average. Instead, a range of values are considered healthy. Test values that fall far outside this range may be indicative of a health problem and merit follow-up.

Beware of the "Lake Wobegon effect"

Lake Wobegon is a fictional Minnesota town featured on the National Public Radio show "A Prairie Home Companion." Garrison Keillor, the show's host, concludes each segment about the town by saying, "Lake Wobegon, where all the women are strong; all the men are good looking, and all the children are above average." It is a joke, of course, but some people really seem to think that everyone should be above average. For example, newspaper articles may bemoan the fact that so many of the students in local schools have scored below average on examinations. Obviously, we want all students to succeed, but it is a simple mathematical fact that if all the scores are added up and divided by the number of students to calculate the average, some students must score below average. In fact, if the distribution of scores is not strangely skewed, half of students will have below average scores. Only in Lake Wobegon can all the students be above average. On the other hand, note that even outside Lake Wobegon, it is mathematically possible for all students to exceed a specific predetermined score, such as a "level of proficiency." Of course, in drawing conclusions about what students have learned, it is important to know how the level of proficiency was set.

For comparisons expressed as a percentage, ask "percent of what?"

Advertisers often claim that their product is X percent, or X times, better, faster acting, or more powerful. For example, they may claim that a conditioner leaves hair 60 percent softer. Assuming that softness can even be objectively measured, it is critical to ask "softer than what?" Is hair 60 percent softer than when no conditioner is used? Is it 60 percent softer than when the cheapest brand of conditioner is used, or when the leading brand of conditioner is used? Similarly, claims are often made that spending, taxes, or inflation have increased or decreased by a certain percentage. To interpret those claims meaningfully, it is important to know more about how the figures were calculated. Over what time period has the change occurred? Is spending being calculated in terms of dollar amounts, or dollar amounts corrected for inflation? We often unconsciously decide what is being compared, because our brains try to make sense of incomplete information. So it is essential to stop and ask ourselves what information has actually been provided, and whether or not it is sufficient.

Reframe losses as gains or gains as losses

A snack with the label "99% natural" seems more appealing than it would if labeled "1% unnatural." A frozen dinner labeled "75% fat free" would sell better than it would with the label "25% fat." The less appealing labeling option is just as accurate as the more appealing option. It also makes us reflect more about what we might be eating. Similarly, bets sound less appealing when framed in terms of the chances of losing or the amount of money one might lose, rather than the chances of winning or the amount of money one could win. Medical procedures may sound scarier when presented in terms of the risk of dying, rather than the likelihood of coming through unscathed. Therefore, it is a useful exercise to recompute losses in terms of gains or gains in terms of losses.

Determine whether there is a context that may explain an observation

Often when we hear that the number of people diagnosed with a disease is on the rise, we imagine that there is something going on in the environment, such as pollution, that is affecting people's health. However, the explanation is sometimes much simpler. For example, the number of people diagnosed with Alzheimer's disease in the United States is climbing steadily. The rise in the numbers of Alzheimer's patients is considerably less mysterious when considered in the context of the fact that the U.S. population is aging. Although the simplest explanation may not be the real explanation, and, as is discussed in detail in Chapter 5, "What Happens If…?," there are many caveats to determining the cause of something, it is useful to pay attention to any context that could potentially explain an observation.

Adequate context and a thorough discussion of pros and cons are often absent in reports about science and political discussions about science. Nonetheless, how to put things in context is something that can be learned. With practice, it becomes natural to get in the habit of stepping back from an article or sound bite to find the big picture context. For different issues, various combinations of contexts will likely be relevant. Table 4.2 illustrates, for one issue, the kinds of critical questions that can be generated based on a knowledge of the different types of possible contexts.

Table 4.2 Putting health care spending in context

"$2 trillion is spent on health care in the U.S. each year"	
Type of context	**Relevant question**
Compare courses of action to other courses of action.	How much does health care spending compare to defense spending?
Put findings in a geographical context.	How does the amount of money spent on health care in America compare to the amount of money spent on health care by Canada, Australia, and western European nations?
Consider the historical context.	How has health care spending changed over time?
Express figures on a comprehensible scale.	How much is spent per person on health care?
Qualify the figures according to the conditions under which they hold true.	What counts as health care? Are prescription drugs counted? Does this include spending on addiction treatment/rehabilitation programs?

Table 4.2   continued

"$2 trillion is spent on health care in the U.S. each year"	
Type of context	**Relevant question**
Ask how the numbers being cited compare to "normal."	None.
Be careful not to be misled by averages.	Is the per capita spending on health care fairly evenly distributed, or do people with certain disorders, people in certain income groups, or people in certain age groups use most of the health care dollars while people in other groups use very little?
For comparisons expressed as a percentage, ask "percent of what?"	If the claim is that health care spending has increased X percent, is that over the past month, year, decade? Does it take inflation into account?
Reframe losses as gains or gains as losses.	How much does each dollar spent on prevention reduce the need to spend on treatment?
Determine whether there is a context that may explain an observation.	If claims are made that health care spending has increased over the years, is it simply because population size has increased? Is it because the baby boomers are aging? Is the increase the result of inflation? That is, does the increase hold up even after it has been corrected for inflation?

Putting it all together

Stakeholders often paint issues in black and white. Yet, when one digs past the surface, messy splotches of color start to emerge. At first, the complexity seems overwhelming, but with the right set of lenses, order can be restored. The color splotches start to organize themselves into layers—themes—and a structure emerges from the chaos. The richness of the pigments remains, but the paint drips flung onto the canvas morph into neat geometric patterns. In other words, the themes of trade-offs and contexts can turn the unmanageableness of Jackson Pollock into the tidiness of Piet Mondrian. The following sidebar presents a checklist summary of Chapters 3 and 4 to act as the lenses that will help you construct order out of chaos.

Checklist to elucidate and evaluate options

- Is the scope of the choice, as presented, too narrow or too broad? For example, are all applications of an innovation being lumped together?

- Are technologies, practices, and policies being compared in isolation, or are the alternatives being compared to one another?

- Have all the risks and benefits (environmental, human health, economic, ethical) been identified?

- Do the long-term and short-term benefits differ?

- Is an appropriate context being used to evaluate claims about risks and benefits? For example, is there a relevant geographical or historical context for comparison?

- Is it possible to re-express numbers to clarify their meaning (identify a comprehensible scale, compare them to normal, determine their median and range, clarify the meaning of a percentage, or translate losses into gains)? Do the numbers need to be qualified according to the conditions under which they hold true?

Choose the appropriate scope of comparison

If a technology has many facets, it may be necessary to narrow the scope of your comparison. For example, genetically engineered crops come in many different varieties, with different risks and benefits. Therefore, it is necessary to consider the risks and benefits on a crop-by-crop basis rather than lumping all genetically engineered crops into the same category. Similarly, a particular technology may have many uses. For some of those uses, the risks may be more substantial than the benefits, or vice versa.

Find the right basis for comparison

When we are looking to replace one thing with something else, we need to be fully informed about the risks and benefits of the new selection with respect to the old. How does the technology, policy, or practice being considered compare with other technologies, policies, or practices? The

choice is not an either/or decision of using or not using a particular technology, policy, or practice. Instead, the choice of adopting something is
always a choice between alternatives. The choice may not be presented
this way, but the option that is not articulated is the *status quo*. In other
words, one of the options is to keep things the way they are. Therefore,
the advantages and disadvantages of the *status quo* must always be taken
into consideration when considering a new alternative.

Consider different themes of tradeoffs

Claims are often about a single risk or benefit, but we need to know what
is being traded off for what. How could the environment be affected?
How could that decision impact human health and comfort? What are
the economic consequences of making a particular decision? The tradeoffs of a choice may be within a single theme, or they may cut across different themes. In many issues, the tradeoffs initially appear to be within
a single theme, but further investigation reveals that aspects of the issue
fall under the other themes.

Think about how the implications of a decision may change over time

For each theme of tradeoff, we need to understand not only the short-
term effects of making a particular decision but also the possible long-
term effects. The long-term effects may be difficult to identify and
quantify, but because most decisions have long-term implications, it is
important to make every effort to predict them and consider their possible significance.

Evaluate risks and benefits by placing them in the appropriate contexts

Putting things into context is not just a matter of comparing the available
options. Options used in other geographical locations or other time periods can also be explored. Another method of putting things in context is
re-expressing them in a different way to see whether it changes their
meaning. For example, it may be possible to re-express large numbers to
make them easier to grasp. Numbers should be expressed according the
conditions in which they are true. They can be compared to a predetermined norm. Averages can be re-expressed as a median or majority.

Percentage comparisons can be articulated more carefully. Losses can be re-expressed as gains. Finally, any context that could explain an observation should be noted and considered.

As the controversy about genetically engineered food illustrates, we cannot assume that the information reaching us is a product of a careful analysis of facts in the relevant context. Even media reports that attempt to present an unbiased view of an issue often leave out the comparisons needed for a reader to develop a nuanced perspective. Whether someone is trained in science or not, it is rare for them to have had formal training in how to make balanced decisions about scientific issues. It is a glaring omission from science education. However, everyone is capable of learning the tricks needed to reason critically about scientific issues.

Clearly, the same choice can be made to seem favorable or unfavorable by selectively presenting certain information and omitting other information. For instance, biotechnology companies can claim that genetic engineering is wonderful because it can make food safer by removing certain toxins or allergens. Antibiotech activists can claim that genetically engineering food is a menace because it can lead to herbicide-resistant superweeds. Both of these claims are true under certain circumstances, but they are each only a small part of the story. Putting together the whole story is not just a matter of comparing alternatives to elucidate the pros and cons, but also being able to assess each pro and con according to its importance and likelihood of occurring in a particular situation.

Claims must be dissected, and the evidence supporting them carefully examined. Part of dissecting claims is putting them in context, as discussed in this chapter, but another part is moving from the big picture to the intricate details of what constitutes good evidence in support of a claim. Many claims are about cause and effect—that something caused something else. Proving beyond a reasonable doubt that there exists a direct relationship between two things is challenging. For example, women were once told that taking hormone replacement therapy after menopause would reduce their risk of heart disease. Then came the announcements that hormone replacement therapy increases the risk of heart disease. Puzzling and contradictory claims like these can be unraveled. The next chapter examines what conclusions are merited from what types of evidence, and reveals common errors people make when using evidence to support claims.

5

What happens if...?: distinguish between cause and coincidence

Vitamins Cut Alzheimer's Effect.

—Headline from *BBC News*, January 2004

Taking Vitamin Supplements May Increase Risk of Death, Says Study.

—Headline from *The Guardian*, February 2007

The contradictory claims that come our way on a regular basis can boggle the mind. Although conflict and disagreement can arise about any area of science, it is particularly exasperating with respect to health topics. People trying to make healthy lifestyle choices based on the information that comes to them through the media often end up bewildered and frustrated. They feel disempowered and conclude that it is not worthwhile to pay attention because scientists keep changing their minds anyway. However, many of the contradictory claims we encounter are not debates in the scientific community itself. Instead they result from how the science is interpreted or misinterpreted. Understanding the potential pitfalls in drawing conclusions from scientific studies is key to becoming a critical consumer of scientific information and learning how to interpret conflicting claims. The preceding chapter considered the role of the bigger picture in assessing the meaningfulness of conclusions drawn from particular findings. Now we turn to the nitty-gritty details of the process of drawing conclusions from those findings.

Claims that come to us through the media are frequently presented along with what is meant to be scientific evidence. We consumers of this information are saddled with the task of sifting through evidence and deciding whether it really does adequately support the claims being made. There are many different types of evidence, and each may justify certain conclusions, but not others. The focus of the next three chapters is to learn to identify weaknesses in evidence and to develop an understanding of the caveats involved in making inferences from it. Three main potential pitfalls will be considered. This chapter explores the difficulties in determining that one phenomenon caused another. Chapter 6, "Specific or General," describes why something that is true under certain circumstances may not be true under others. Chapter 7, "Fun Figures," delves into the challenges of interpreting statistical information.

Cause and effect—finding the culprit

Whether it is a disease, global climate change, or the breakdown of a particular technology, there can be a long list of possible causes. A given phenomenon can have multiple interacting causes, and it may take many studies to determine all of them. Furthermore, for ethical or practical reasons, it is not always possible to do an experiment that could pinpoint the cause(s). As a result, scientists also need to rely on nonexperimental data, which provides less direct evidence about the cause of an observation or event than a well-designed experiment. Many intricacies are involved in establishing a link between a cause and an effect.

We all have personal experience trying to determine the cause of something, such as an illness—perhaps getting sick to the stomach after a friend's barbeque. It could have been the potato salad, the egg salad, or that burger that looked a little underdone. Maybe it was not the food, but a touch of heatstroke from being out in the sun all day. Then again, maybe you were coming down with stomach flu all along, and it just happened to coincide with the barbeque. You could poll your friends to find out who ate what and who got sick, but you probably would not find a definitive answer. For instance, even if the egg salad was tainted, it is unlikely that everyone who ate it got sick because people have different levels of resistance to bacteria. In addition, you might find someone who felt ill even though they did not eat any egg salad.

Complex diseases, including cancer, heart disease, and Alzheimer's, are even more difficult to understand because they are caused by multiple interacting factors, and because there is often a significant amount of time between the exposure to some risk factor, for instance a toxin, and the onset of the disease. To see whether a specific risk factor causes a disease, epidemiologists—researchers who study the spread and control of diseases—compare the occurrence of the disease in populations that have been exposed to that risk factor and those that have not been exposed. Since it is unethical to deliberately expose people to a substance that may cause illness, epidemiologists must study existing populations of people exposed and not exposed.

Epidemiologists perform many different types of studies, but two types most commonly cited in the media are **retrospective** and **prospective** observational studies. In a retrospective study, a group of people who have a particular disease and a group of people who do not have that disease are questioned about their lifestyles and/or exposure to certain substances. The researchers may also use historical accounts, medical records, or other information to try to determine an individual's exposure. Differences between the groups may provide insight into what triggered the disease. The greatest weakness of this type of study is **recall bias**—people with a disease are more likely to remember, correctly or incorrectly, having been exposed to certain things that they think could have caused their disease. In a prospective study, people who have been exposed to a factor thought to cause (or combat) a disease are followed over time and compared to people who have not been exposed to that factor. For example, those exposed to radioactive fallout from the atomic bomb dropped on Hiroshima have been followed over the years to determine the fallout's effects on cancer rates. One obvious disadvantage of prospective studies is that it usually takes many years, even decades, of gathering data to conclude that a factor does or does not cause a disease. Both prospective and retrospective epidemiological studies can provide important insights into factors that may cause disease, or protect from disease, but they need to be interpreted with caution.

Brainstorm other possible causes

To determine whether smoking was a cause of lung cancer, epidemiologists compared rates of lung cancer in smokers versus nonsmokers. Smokers had higher rates of lung cancer than nonsmokers. Could this be taken as conclusive evidence that smoking causes lung cancer? No, because smokers and nonsmokers differ in more than their cigarette habits. One difference is that, on average, poorer people are more likely to be smokers than wealthier people. Poorer people are more likely to live near factories or in inner city neighborhoods with air pollution and higher levels of environmental toxins, factors that would also influence lung cancer rates. On average, poorer people eat less fruits and vegetables than those in higher socioeconomic groups, and antioxidants in fruits and vegetables reduce cancer rates. This interplay of possible causal relationships is shown diagrammatically in Figure 5.1.

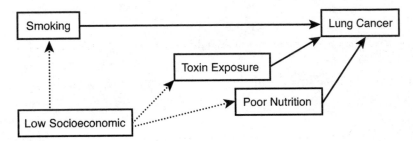

FIGURE 5.1   Factors that must be teased apart to confirm the relationship between smoking and lung cancer

Recognize that nonexperimental findings such as epidemiological observations have caveats

In the smoking example, the initial epidemiological studies were corroborated by experimental studies in animals as well as the elucidation of the mechanism by which specific chemicals in tobacco smoke cause cells to become cancerous. As a result, the relationship between smoking and lung cancer is well accepted by scientists and nonscientists alike. However, epidemiological studies can sometimes be downright misleading. Until recently, women were told by their doctors that hormone replacement therapy (HRT) after menopause would reduce their risk of heart disease. This information was based on studies comparing women who chose to take HRT to those who did not take it. However, the results of the first large, randomized study of HRT painted a very different picture. It found that HRT actually increased the risk of heart disease.

Why were the initial studies wrong? It turns out that the women who *chose* to take HRT tended to be more physically active, more educated, less likely to be obese, and less likely to smoke than other women.

In other words, the women taking HRT were healthier on average to begin with, and less likely to develop heart disease, than the women who did not take HRT. This parallels the smoking example in that the two groups being compared had differences other than the factor (HRT/No HRT) whose effects scientists were trying to understand. However, a major difference between this example and the previous example is that because, unlike smoking, HRT was thought to have health benefits, it was ethical to do an experimental study in which participants were randomly assigned to take or not take HRT.

The headline that began this chapter—that vitamins could protect against Alzheimer's—was also based on an epidemiological study. Unfortunately, the fact that a study was observational rather than experimental is often not clarified until the end of an article, and it is almost never highlighted in the headline. For example, another story about Alzheimer's and supplements, published the same week in the San Diego *Union Tribune*, was titled "Preventing Alzheimer's." It argued that taking high doses of vitamins was safe and could have considerable health benefits. Not until the last line of the article was the reader told that the claims were based on an observational study.

The "Preventing Alzheimer's" article did not reveal anything about the initial differences between the people who chose to take supplements and those who did not. Vitamin supplements are expensive. Maybe the people who took them were wealthier on average than the people who did not. Could the apparent protective effect against Alzheimer's be due to differences in stress or lifestyle factors that relate to income, rather than vitamin supplements? The article does not provide enough information to answer this question. Therefore, the last sentence in the article is the most important. Observational studies (see Figure 5.2) can provide tantalizing leads to follow, but they must be treated with caution. In fact, a study published in the *Journal of the American Medical Association* found that nearly one-third of original research results did not hold up in later studies. Observational studies of patients' lifestyles were the most likely to be later contradicted. Whenever possible, the findings of observational studies are tested in experimental studies (see Figure 5.3). Therefore, to evaluate health claims, a critical consumer of information needs to ask what type of study the claims are based on.

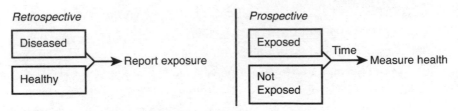

FIGURE 5.2   Observational epidemiological studies

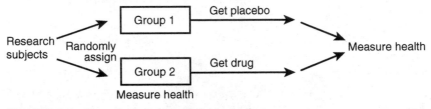

FIGURE 5.3   Experimental or clinical studies

Experimental studies are the best way to determine the cause of something because, in a well-designed experimental study, key variables—such as sex, age, diet, physical activity, and other health factors—can be controlled while examining the variable of interest. Given that the second headline beginning this chapter and the following claim—regarding the health *risks* of high dose supplements—came from a clinical (experimental) study, the safest conclusion is that it may not always be safe or beneficial to take megadoses of vitamins.

> *People taking vitamin A supplements are 16 percent more likely to die than those not taking supplements within the trial period, while beta-carotene and vitamin E supplement-takers are at 7 and 4 percent greater risk.*[1]

High doses of vitamins may be useful under certain conditions, or for some people, but despite the claim in the "Preventing Alzheimer's" article, the current state of scientific knowledge does not suggest it is safe to start popping vitamins like candy.

In medicine, especially in testing new drugs, randomized, double blind, placebo-controlled studies are the norm. In a **randomized** study, subjects are assigned at random to either an experimental (get the drug) or control (get the placebo—an inert, or fake, pill) group. Subjects usually complete questionnaires and may undergo a medical examination.

[1] *New Scientist*, March 3, 2007.

Statistical tests are applied to make sure that the experimental and control groups really are equivalent on key variables at the beginning of an experiment. For example, to test a weight loss drug, it is important to balance the experimental and control groups for subjects' initial levels of obesity and health factors, such as diabetes, that are related to obesity. **Double blind** means that neither the experimental subjects nor the doctors who are evaluating the patients know who is getting the drug and who is getting a placebo. Doctors' preconceived notions about what a particular medicine will do can influence their assessment of a patient's health, which is why it is best that the physician evaluating a patient's condition in a clinical trial be ignorant of what treatment the patient is receiving.

Placebos are crucial because when patients think they are getting a drug for a particular ailment, even if they are not, they are more likely to report improvements in their condition. Patients may not merely think they are better; they may really get better through the power of positive thinking. The placebo effect is well known, but there is also a less familiar **nocebo effect**, in which patients may be more likely to report symptoms that they believe are side effects of a drug. Every day we all suffer from minor aches and pains—a kink in the neck, a headache, an upset stomach—but do not spend time worrying that they might be something serious. But if we have a reason to attribute the symptoms to something serious, we may become fixated on them. The worrying may even make the symptoms worse. Thus, first-year medical students often convince themselves that they are suffering from many of the illnesses covered in their textbooks. A few people concerned that their health is being affected by hazardous material at a nearby industry may set off an "epidemic" among neighbors panicking that their own unexplained aches and pains are a sign that they are being poisoned by toxins in the environment. Likewise, patients who read the side effect warnings on their new drug may become more conscious of symptoms such as an ache in the lower back (What if it is a sign of kidney failure?) or a leg cramp (What if it is a blood clot?) and report them to their doctor.

Relative risk

Nearly every news report about medical and health research warns against something that will increase the risk of stroke, heart attack, cancer, and so on. They never say that anyone will ever actually suffer any of the consequences. It's always an increased risk of experiencing the malady. If the "risk of getting lung cancer" is 50 percent greater, does that mean that 50 percent more people will actually get lung cancer?

Relative risk is used to assess the relationship between a possible risk factor (for example, smoking) and a disease (for example, lung cancer). It is defined as the ratio of the disease rate (for example, the number of lung cancer cases per 100,000 people) among those exposed to the risk factor, to the disease rate among those not exposed.

Just because the disease rate is higher among people exposed to a possible risk factor does not prove it causes the disease. Genetics, socioeconomic status, nutrition, exercise habits, and so forth also affect the risk of many diseases.

A 50 percent greater risk of getting a disease may translate to 50 percent more people getting that disease, but only if all other things are equal in the population scientists have studied and the population about which they are making predictions.

Be skeptical of anecdotal evidence

The placebo effect is one reason it is dangerous to rely on anecdotes or testimonials as evidence. For example, about one-third of people with depression feel better when they are taking inert pills that they have been led to think are medicine. Many ailments respond to treatment with a placebo. So if someone claims to feel better as a result of taking a new nutritional supplement, or purported remedy for some ailment, the individual may genuinely believe the pills are making a difference, but the effect may be on the mind rather than on the body.

The placebo effect is not just limited to medications and nutritional supplements. People often make incorrect assumptions about the effects of other types of lifestyle changes as well. For example, they may assume that getting a regular massage is helping them lose weight, when their weight loss can be explained by subtle dietary changes they made in conjunction with beginning massage therapy. There is evidence to suggest that when people make a small change in their daily routine, they may consciously or subconsciously make other changes as well. In one study, people were asked to think of a new adjective each day, such as "extraverted," "content," or "reflective," and behave in the manner described by that adjective. Although dieting was not part of the study, participants lost weight, indicating that they had made additional lifestyle changes as a result of the experiment. Therefore, it is risky to trust an anecdote claiming that a drug or lifestyle change caused some desired (or undesired) result because the result may be due to a coincident change. Furthermore, the placebo effect is not just a problem in health studies. It can be an issue whenever subjective judgment comes into play, such as in assessing the performance of a vehicle after the addition of a fuel enhancer, or the difference in effectiveness between a generic and a brand name cleaning solution.

Understand how combining multiple forms of data can strengthen conclusions

Although experimental studies have many advantages over nonexperimental studies, they have drawbacks and uncertainties of their own. One problem is noncompliance—an experimental subject fails to adhere to the experimental protocol. Subjects may not take the medication according to the assigned schedule or doses. They may fail to follow the diet assigned to them. They also may not report truthfully about their failures, either because of social pressure, or because they do not want to be kicked out of a study that provides them with financial compensation. Another problem is that it is expensive and difficult to run an experimental study for as long as it may take to assess the long-term effects of taking a drug, following a diet plan, or making some other lifestyle change. Sometimes experimental results are inconclusive because it is not possible to control every factor that could affect the outcome of an experiment, or, as was discussed in Chapter 1, "Potions, Plot, Personalities," there are outstanding questions about the technologies used to perform the experiment.

In addition, it is not always feasible to perform an experimental study. Ethical limitations on experimental studies in the health sciences have already been mentioned. Technical and practical limitations also arise. For example, the sheer number of cells in the human brain makes it difficult to determine how learning a particular task alters connections between individual nerve cells. Certain scientific problems, particularly those involving events that happened in the past—such as the big bang, evolution of a species, or the origin of life—are not very amenable to study by experimentation. As a result, the study of complex scientific problems usually entails combining multiple types of data to strengthen the conclusions that can be drawn.

In the case of evolution, for example, scientists can study fossils and make predictions about species, or "missing links," that may have once existed. The subsequent discovery of a fossil with the predicted characteristics, as occurred in the whale evolution example discussed in Chapter 1, is considered good support for scientists' hypotheses about the ancestral lineage of a particular species. Fossil evidence comes to mind for most people when they think of evolution, but an obvious weakness is that fossil finds are sporadic. Another line of evidence used by evolutionary biologists is the genetic variation between existing species (and extinct species when genetic evidence is available) that has led to specific adaptations. Scientists may choose a particular trait, such as differences in coat coloration of subspecies of mice living in different environments. By comparing the genes that control the trait in different populations, scientists determine whether the trait can be traced back to a common ancestor or arose independently in different populations.

The fossil record and genetic studies help evolutionary biologists show how organisms are related to each other and that adaptations correspond to specific genetic changes. However, even combined with information about past climate, sea levels, atmospheric composition, and so on, these findings do not give adequate insight into the mechanisms of natural selection—how the environmental conditions made it possible for individuals with certain genetic characteristics to have more offspring. Studies of bacteria and other organisms that reproduce very quickly can provide insight into these processes. Scientists can expose these organisms to different environmental conditions and watch evolution in action. Therefore, while in isolation, each of these forms of evidence—the fossil record, genetic studies, and experiments with microorganisms—is limited in terms of the conclusions that can be drawn, together they buttress one another and permit scientists to draw firmer conclusions about what caused the observed changes.

Global climate change is another area where many forms of evidence must be combined in drawing conclusions. A single experiment could not be designed to test global warming because too many factors must to be taken into consideration, and it is impossible to accurately recreate global conditions on a small scale. Instead, the results of different lines of investigation, pursued by many scientists working in different fields, are pieced together. The diversity of the data being used to understand climate change is not usually evident in media reports about it. Examples of the kinds of data being used to understand climate change are shown in Table 5.1.

TABLE 5.1 Evidence being studied to understand global climate change

Past global temperatures and climate	Present global temperatures and weather patterns
Annual growth rings of trees	Satellite temperature measurements
Past sea levels recorded in sedimentary rock	Land-based temperatures
Glacier movements recorded in rock and land formations	Ocean temperatures
Biodiversity (e.g., changes in elevation at which a particular species grew)	Changes in yearly freeze/melt cycles of rivers, lakes, Arctic passages, and glacier/ice cap melting
	Yearly patterns of rainfall, severe weather conditions, etc.
	Biodiversity (e.g., changes in elevation at which a particular species grows)

Past atmosphere	Present atmosphere
Gases trapped in ice cores	Sampling at various altitudes
Ratio of isotopes—heavier or lighter atoms—of carbon in tree rings	Measurements of isotopes of carbon to determine anthropogenic contribution of CO_2

TABLE 5.1   continued

Amplifying and mitigating factors in global climate change and weather patterns

Temperature effects on photosynthesis (CO_2 uptake by plants)	Solar cycles (sunspots, etc.)
Temperature effects on decomposition rates of organic matter in soil (CO_2 release)	Reflectivity of ice versus ground and changes in Earth's ice coverage over time
Likelihood of methane release from permafrost and ocean sediments due to warming	Impact of melting ice on ocean salinity and resultant changes in ocean currents
Temperature influences on the ability of the ocean to sequester CO_2	Volcanic activity
How atmospheric particles interfere with sunlight reaching earth	Shorter-term weather oscillation data (La Niña, El Niño)
How clouds affect daytime and nighttime temperatures	Tilt and orbit of the earth
What affects cloud formation (including atmospheric particles)	

Recognize that a plausible mechanism is key to linking a cause and an effect

Anthropogenic—man-made—greenhouse gases are not the only possible cause of climate change. Changes in global climate can be caused by small shifts in the tilt of the earth's axis, variations in the earth's orbit around the sun, volcanic activity, and fluctuations in the sun's energy output. Therefore, while the recent warming trend closely parallels the sharp increase in carbon dioxide production that started with the Industrial Revolution, this relationship, or **correlation**, is not proof that the observed increase in atmospheric carbon dioxide is the cause of the warming. In fact, scientists would be much more skeptical about the role of greenhouse gases if there were no plausible mechanism to explain how the increase in the concentrations of these gases in the atmosphere could lead to global warming.

The mechanism by which greenhouse gases cause global warming has to do with the difference in energy between the visible radiation that passes through Earth's atmosphere from the sun, and the infrared radiation that is reflected from Earth back into space. The reflected infrared radiation is less energetic than the incoming radiation and more likely to be absorbed by the carbon dioxide molecules in the atmosphere. When the carbon dioxide re-emits the radiation, some of it is sent back toward Earth, rather than released into space. Thus, carbon dioxide and other greenhouse gases act something like the glass in a greenhouse to keep heat in. The **greenhouse effect** is a normal process that protects our planet from the temperature extremes characteristic of planets lacking an atmosphere. However, an increase in the amount of greenhouse gases may cause the warming to get out of control. Because of this plausible mechanism, combined with evidence of global warming, including land and ocean temperature measurements, documentation of melting ice and glaciers and certain biodiversity changes, and the ruling out of other possible major causes of climate change, the Intergovernmental Panel on Climate Change (IPCC) reported in 2007 that: "Most of the observed increase in globally averaged temperatures since the mid-20th century is very likely due to the observed increase in anthropogenic greenhouse gas concentrations." However, the IPCC statement may not be the final word on global climate change, which continues to be an active area of research.

Multiple causes and effects come into play in the global climate change controversy, especially in estimating the severity of the warming and its consequences. For example, initial temperature changes can influence cloud formation, photosynthesis rates in plants, and decomposition of organic matter, which in turn, by reflecting sunlight and sequestering or releasing carbon dioxide, can mitigate or worsen the warming. Understanding the mechanisms of each of these processes is key to developing accurate computer models to estimate how much warming could occur. Since so many factors can amplify or mitigate global warming (refer to the bottom row of Table 5.1), it is challenging to make firm predictions about future temperatures. The global climate change controversy is not unique in this respect; determining the causes of diseases, declines in biodiversity, and many other phenomena often requires understanding a network of interrelated mechanisms.

Mechanisms are critical in science. Sometimes, as discussed in Chapter 1, scientists place so much emphasis on mechanisms that interesting scientific ideas are ignored because there is no mechanism to explain them yet. In making sense of claims in the media, it is important to try to find a middle ground. Just because there is no known mechanism linking a cause and effect does not necessarily mean they are not linked. For instance, the active ingredient in aspirin was known to treat headaches decades before anyone had the slightest idea how it worked. However, a close look at a purported mechanism can often reveal suspect claims. For example, manufacturers of "antiaging" face creams would like consumers to believe that creams containing collagen make you look younger by adding collagen to your skin. The idea that collagen—a large structural protein—would penetrate deep into the skin and integrate with the collagen produced in the body warrants much skepticism.

Advertisements for various brands of bottled water claim that the water has better hydration properties because the water molecules in it have been broken into smaller clusters than are found in regular water. These expensive, supposedly high-tech brands of water sell well at health food stores. Yet, consumers would do well to hold onto their pocketbooks. If true, the finding that the structure of water can be altered in a new way would be a major scientific breakthrough that would be published in a top scientific journal. Anyone with a basic understanding of chemistry would find the claim highly suspect if they encountered it for the first time in an advertisement rather than in a scientific paper. Therefore, when in doubt, it is worth asking someone with relevant scientific training whether a claim about a mechanism seems realistic, or whether there could be a plausible mechanism to explain a purported observation.

Given the importance of learning to recognize potential risks, such as foods that make us sick, behaviors that make our acquaintances angry, and physical dangers in our environment, it is not surprising that when two phenomena are linked in time, we are quick to conclude that there is a causal relationship between them. Unfortunately, our propensity to jump to conclusions can make us overlook the real cause. After all, as illustrated in Figure 5.4, two factors can be linked in time by coincidence; they can appear linked because there is a third factor that causes each of them; and they can be wrongly associated by a poorly designed experiment that allowed an experimenter or experimental subject to introduce confounds, for example, by not accounting for the placebo effect.

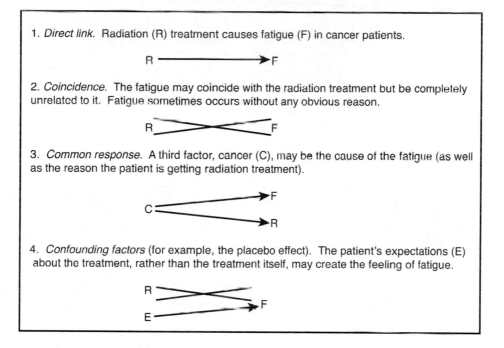

1. *Direct link.* Radiation (R) treatment causes fatigue (F) in cancer patients.

2. *Coincidence.* The fatigue may coincide with the radiation treatment but be completely unrelated to it. Fatigue sometimes occurs without any obvious reason.

3. *Common response.* A third factor, cancer (C), may be the cause of the fatigue (as well as the reason the patient is getting radiation treatment).

4. *Confounding factors* (for example, the placebo effect). The patient's expectations (E) about the treatment, rather than the treatment itself, may create the feeling of fatigue.

FIGURE 5.4   Cause and effect links and complications

To avoid being misled about the cause of something, it is important to consider and rule out other possible causes. Whenever two groups are being compared, brainstorm what might realistically be different about the groups. Make sure studies have been controlled for appropriate factors. Ask whether there are multiple forms of data that point to the same cause. Is there a mechanism that could plausibly link two phenomena? A plausible mechanism makes it much more likely that they are linked by cause rather than coincidence. However, even when it can be safely concluded that one phenomenon has caused another, questions arise about the conditions under which the relationship will hold true. For this reason, even well-designed experimental studies have their limitations. Just because some factor causes something to occur in one situation does not mean that under different circumstances the same link would exist. Determining how broadly conclusions about cause can be applied is the focus of the next chapter.

6

Specific or general: recognize how broadly the conclusions from a study may be applied

When It Comes to Aspirin, Men and Women Are Not Equal: Aspirin acts differently in women.
—Headline from *American Journal of Nursing*, June 2005

Race-based Medicine?
—Headline from *The Scientist*, November 2007

Controversy Regarding Screening Mammography Under Age 50: To screen or not to screen.
    Headline from *Radiology*, June 1993

Experience tells us that our observations and the effects of our actions vary according to at least four factors. First, there are individual differences. For example, differences among friends and family members mean that we get a wide range of responses to our ideas, jokes, cooking, interior decorating, and lifestyle choices. Second, there are differences of locale. The country and community in which we live determine social norms. Geography and climate have a big impact on what animals and plants live in a region and what types of diseases are prevalent. Third, even with a particular individual or a particular location, conditions vary. Individuals have different moods and different states of health and well-being. In a given location, weather conditions vary from year to year, and can influence disease outbreaks, crop yields, and so on. Finally, there are time variations. Fashions and fads in dress, architecture, vehicles, and

popular culture vary over time. Laws change over time. Natural landscapes change over time through erosion and maturation of ecosystems.
Therefore, when using evidence to inform decisions, it is essential to
consider whether findings from one situation will hold up in another.
Consider some examples where differences in individuals, locations,
conditions, and time come into play.

Individuals: consider whether a result collected in one test population applies to another

No matter how well a study is designed, its results cannot automatically
be applied beyond the population studied. Age, gender, socioeconomic
status, racial and ethnic background, level of education, and prior health
are some of the factors that affect how people respond to diseases, medications, dietary recommendations, new legislation, social programs, and
so on. Differences in populations must be taken into consideration in
drawing conclusions from epidemiological studies and experiments.
Such differences are one reason, in addition to the placebo effect, that
anecdotes are untrustworthy. We are all different in one way or another
and may not respond to an intervention the same way as the person
described in the anecdote.

Even with a large test population, failure to take population differences into account can result in conclusions that are completely incorrect. For example, doctors recommend aspirin for both men and women
at high risk of heart disease. However, recent studies have shown that,
contrary to what it does for men, aspirin does not reduce the risk of heart
disease for women under 65. Similarly, one drug to treat high blood pressure demonstrated effectiveness in African Americans, but not other
racial groups. Age is also a factor. For instance, there is little controversy
that getting regular mammograms is important for women over 50. On
the other hand, there is significant controversy over whether women
between 40 and 50 should get regular mammograms. Mammograms are
the best tool available for detecting early stage breast cancer, but many
medical professionals argue that the risk of mammograms—from the X-
rays and the false positives that result in needless biopsies—outweigh the
benefits for younger women without a family history of premenopausal
breast cancer. Not only are younger women at lower risk for breast
cancer, their breast tissue is denser, which makes it more difficult to
interpret the mammogram.

Many scientific studies use organisms other than humans and are often carried out with the goal of eventually applying the findings to humans. Usually such studies are not simply a substitution for research that could not ethically be performed on humans. Controlling variables such as diet and lifestyle is much simpler with laboratory organisms. Compliance—taking a medication according to the schedule assigned—is also much easier to ensure. By far the greatest advantage is the ability to relatively easily compare groups of organisms with particular genetic characteristics. It is even possible to breed varieties of organisms that lack a particular gene to better understand that gene's function. The results of such experiments provide important, sometimes surprising, information about the role of particular genes. For instance, not infrequently, mice lacking a gene thought to be required for a particular function, such as the development of the nervous system, appear healthy and normal. The fact that removing the gene had no discernable effect means that either the scientists were wrong about the function of the gene, or that there is redundancy—another gene is able to perform the same function.

Mice are just one species of what scientists refer to as **model organisms**. Other common model organisms are fruit flies (more formally referred to as *Drosophila*), nematode worms (more formally referred to as *C. Elegans*), bacteria (especially *E. coli*), frogs, zebra fish, and rats. Scientists have a good understanding of the life cycles of all these organisms and can easily breed and care for them in a laboratory. Furthermore, each species of model organism has its own particular advantages. Fruit flies, nematode worms, and bacteria are relatively easy to manipulate genetically. Frogs and zebra fish are vertebrates like us, but their fertilized eggs are transparent and develop outside the mother's body, making it easier to observe the early stages in development. Mice and rats' physiology is sufficiently similar to our own to have made them the animals of choice for testing the effects of new medications before proceeding to clinical trials on humans.

When I was conducting research with fruit flies, people often asked me why on earth I would want to study flies. Remarkably, fruit flies tell us a great deal about human diseases as well as normal human development. For example, the genes that pattern the body, which make sure your head does not end up where your chest should be, were initially discovered in flies, but this family of genes is responsible for patterning the human body as well. In a dramatic demonstration of just how great is the similarity between some fly and human genes, scientists removed from flies the gene that initiates eye development, without which the fly fails to develop eyes, and replaced it with the human gene that initiates eye development in humans. The flies developed perfectly normal eyes. The flies developed fly eyes, not human eyes, because the gene that was replaced is responsible for *initiating* eye development. Other genes decide the shape, size, and other characteristics of the eye.

By studying mutant flies, scientists can determine what goes wrong genetically in certain diseases in humans. It is possible to mutate a large number of fruit flies by exposing them to chemicals that damage their DNA. The damage to the DNA will happen at random. Some flies will die; some flies will appear normal, and the remainder will have a variety of mutations. Researchers can then choose flies with defects that they are interested in studying, such as visual problems, and determine what genes have been mutated. They can determine the DNA sequence of the mutated gene and find out whether a similar gene is present in humans. They would want to know whether mutations in the gene are responsible for genetic disorders in humans, such as inherited visual disorders. Many methods and tools have been perfected for locating a mutated gene and determining its DNA sequence in flies. So, even though it may seem backward to look for a gene in flies first, and then determine whether the gene is mutated in a specific human disorder, it can be much more efficient than searching for a mutated gene in humans without knowing anything about its DNA sequence.

Finding a gene involved in a human genetic disorder is a challenging process that usually takes years of work by many research groups. Also, for any complex process, such as the development of the visual system, multiple genes will be involved. It is tricky to tease apart the role played by each gene. However, the use of model organisms that are relatively easy to manipulate genetically has led to the discovery of genes implicated in many inherited disorders in humans.

Of course, there are disadvantages of using model organisms. They make certain types of experiments possible, but what is learned from model organisms cannot automatically be applied to humans. In fact, what is true for one model organism does not always hold true for another (even closely related) model organism. For example, the dose of the chemical dioxin that kills a hamster is thousands of times higher than the dose that kills a guinea pig. Variation between organisms makes it important to have supporting data, either experimental or epidemiological, in humans when drawing conclusions about what a study means. This is why, for example, a drug that eliminates tumors in mice still has to go through clinical trials in humans. The goal of the clinical trials is not only to determine whether the drug will work in humans but also to identify any side effects in humans that do not occur, or are not easily identified, in mice. Unfortunately, it is not unusual for potential treatments to fail to live up to the promise they showed in animal studies.

If an experiment provides strong evidence that the link between a cause and an effect is real, it is important to consider whether the results based on the population used in the experiment apply to the general population. Is there sufficient evidence that results from an animal study will apply to humans? Do studies of white men apply to women or men of other racial groups? Will a drug that works well in adult populations also work in children? These questions may require many years of research to answer, and, in the interim, assumptions are made about the applicability of the results to populations beyond the population studied. For example, pharmaceutical companies may choose not to test a drug on children; however, doctors may prescribe the drug to children. Doing so essentially makes those children experimental subjects in the course of trying to help them. This occurred in the case of certain antidepressants. Over time, evidence (albeit weak, as discussed in Chapter 8, "Society's Say") arose that in some children and teens, the antidepressants might increase suicide risk. Following a review of these findings, the U.S. Food and Drug Administration mandated that labels be placed on the antidepressants to warn parents of their risks. Being aware that results may not apply to all populations should make you more skeptical of claims of "cure-alls," help you understand why certain therapies may not work for you, and help you decide how much weight to assign to new scientific findings in making your own lifestyle choices.

Locale: consider how applicable studies of one community or geographical region are to other locales

Just as studies of one population may not apply to other populations, studies carried out in one setting may not be applicable to other settings. In the control of infectious diseases, locale plays an important role in determining which solutions will be successful. For example, different approaches to controlling malaria—which kills between one million and three million people each year, primarily in Africa—work best in different communities. Malaria is caused by a parasite called a *plasmodium*, which is carried by mosquitoes. There are several ways to help prevent people from getting bitten by mosquitoes: having people stay indoors between dusk and dawn when mosquitoes are most active, cleaning up standing water where mosquitoes can breed, having people sleep under bed nets, spraying pesticides, and introducing natural predators of mosquitoes. Some of these preventative measures only work if there is a communitywide effort, which requires adequate leadership and a spirit of cooperation. Furthermore, some measures, such as cleaning up trash and other items that can hold water, significantly reduce mosquito populations only in certain geographical regions. If there are few natural lakes and ponds, then cleaning up objects that hold water can make a difference in the mosquito population. If a community is surrounded by marshes, then other measures, such as introducing fish that eat mosquito larvae, would be critical.

Other domains where locale needs to be considered are agriculture and land management. For example, some genetically modified crops that in northern states gave higher yields than their conventional counterparts, fared more poorly in hotter southern states. In general, crops must be selected and/or tailored for particular soils and climatic conditions. Therefore, any conclusions drawn about a crop may not apply outside the geographical range in which it was tested. Similarly, best practices for forest management vary according to the type of forest, geographical conditions, and proximity to housing developments. For fire control, thinning trees and clearing underbrush might make sense for forests near human dwellings but does not have the same benefits in old-growth forests in isolated areas.

When considering a problem solution that has been tested in another situation, it is therefore important to examine the similarities and differences between the test environment and the environment in which the solution is being applied. One-size-fits-all policies should be regarded with healthy skepticism. Also, failures should be carefully examined rather than swept under the carpet, as is sometimes the tendency of politicians and others. Important lessons can be learned when a solution fails in a particular environment because such failures can reveal what factors need to be in place for the solution to be successful.

Conditions: consider the possible effects of a change in conditions on experimental findings or their applicability

Both man-made and natural conditions are dynamic. Landscapes change via erosion, melting of glaciers, earthquakes, volcanic activity, maturation of ecosystems, and damage to ecosystems by fire or human activity. El Niño, La Niña, and other weather systems can lead to drought and floods, even in areas that do not usually experience extreme weather. Changes in conditions can have wide-ranging consequences. For example, global warming seems to be allowing malaria to spread to geographical regions previously free of the disease. Therefore, changes in conditions need to be considered when deciding whether evidence collected under one set of conditions applies in others, and solutions to problems need to change dynamically to respond to changes in conditions.

The cause of what appears to be a single problem can turn out to be the result of multiple changes in conditions. For example, at a conference in 1989, scientists realized that, all around the world, frogs and other amphibians were disappearing. The discovery led to a search for the changes in conditions that were decimating amphibian populations. The search continues to this day, and it appears that many different changes in conditions play a role in amphibian declines in different regions. Where there is water run-off from cropland, pesticides are suspected to play a role. In many places, habitat destruction is causing the declines. The construction of roads that divide habitats is another problem because frogs and their kin get squashed while trying to migrate back to breeding ponds.

Other changes in conditions act in less direct ways. For example, in one region, lower rainfall resulted in shallower ponds, which allowed more ultraviolet radiation from the sun to reach frogs' eggs. Eggs that were exposed to more ultraviolet radiation turned out to be more susceptible to fungal infections. Careful observation and experimentation are required to unravel complex chains of effects like these. For example, scientists had to determine whether it was ultraviolet radiation, or some other consequence of ponds being shallower, that was leading to frog mortality. To find out, they compared different groups of eggs allowed to develop at different depths that were protected or not protected with ultraviolet-blocking filters. When protected with filters to block ultraviolet radiation, eggs left to develop in shallower water developed normally, unlike those not protected by ultraviolet blocking filters. In other words, shallow water was not itself unhealthy; instead, it was the penetration of ultraviolet radiation that was unhealthy. An appropriate course of action depends on correctly identifying the cause, but it is easy to be misled into thinking that a change in conditions and an occurrence are directly linked. In fact, as this example shows, illustrated in Figure 6.1, the relationship can be subtle and part of a sequence of events that each results from one another.

↓ **Rainfall** ─────────────────────────────────→ ↓**Frogs**

↓ **Rainfall** → ↓ Pond depth → ↑ UV penetration → ↑ Fungal infections → ↓ **Frogs**

FIGURE 6.1   It's raining frogs: the intricate relationship between lower rainfall and frog declines

In addition to changes in conditions at a particular location, conditions change within an individual. For example, pregnancy, age, stress, diet, or other lifestyle changes can influence how well a medical treatment might work. Family issues and financial situations also change, making it more or less likely that certain solutions to problems will be effective. Changing conditions can be a source of frustration when a product or course of action that worked in the past ceases to work. Careful analyses may be needed to track down what has changed and find a new solution.

Time: consider whether findings would be influenced by time, either the period of history or the duration of the study

Of course, evidence collected in one time period may not apply in others because of changing conditions. For example, since the 1800s, infant and maternal mortality has dramatically decreased in developed countries as a result of improvements in hygiene and nutrition. However, as introduced in Chapter 3, "Decisions, Decisions," time is an important factor on its own, independent of conditions. Specifically, habits or practices that are safe in the short term may not be safe in the long term. For example, a pesticide may work well for a few seasons, but over time insects often develop resistance to pesticides. The effects of agricultural practices that fail to adequately replenish minerals in the soil slowly accumulate over time and result in land unfit for growing crops. Withdrawing more water from aquifers than is being replaced by rain results in **subsidence**—the decrease in elevation of the land surface. Subsidence is often not obvious in the short term but can be dramatic over the long term. For example, some areas of California's San Joaquin Valley have dropped 30 feet in 75 years due to the excessive removal of ground water.

Medicine is another area in which time plays an important role. The health effects of a drug, nutritional supplement, or other substance may be dramatically different in the short term than in the long term. However, it is impractical to evaluate the very long-term health effects of something in humans before putting it on the market. Not only would clinical trials that ran for decades be prohibitively costly, but it would mean that decades would be added to the time it takes to develop and approve a new drug. Therefore, if there are negative long-term effects of taking a particular drug, those effects are not detected until patients and doctors start reporting them. For example, the blockbuster arthritis drug Vioxx was withdrawn in 2004 after evidence accumulated that it could cause heart attacks in some patients.

When evaluating claims about products or policies, it is important to assess whether the evidence being used to bolster the claims is up-to-date and whether there is data about long-term effects. Advertisers may point out the immediate benefits of a product and imply that the effects are lasting, or only get better with time. On the contrary, the product may lose its effectiveness over time, or side effects may only materialize over time. Similarly, the argument that a policy worked in the past and therefore will work in the present may be completely bogus. Urbanization, globalization, population growth, new economic models, and changing social norms are all factors that have to be taken into consideration when extrapolating a policy from one era to another.

Clearly, sorting out cause and effect is a complex task. It begins with an attempt to elucidate all the possible variables that might cause the result observed. The task is tricky because multiple competing factors may work independently, in combination, or in sequence, and the critical factors may be different for different people or in different situations. Researchers try to isolate one factor to test its role in causing something, but in the real world it is challenging to separate one factor from another or to design a test that takes every possible factor into consideration. Ultimately, it is the results of multiple studies, often designed differently, that convince researchers of the relationship between a cause and an effect. Still, the results of individual studies come to us via the media, and because the results of the next big study on an issue can be years away, we need to decide whether the information at hand is worth taking into consideration as we make decisions. In addition to understanding the nuances of cause and effect and diversity of situations, deciding on the implications of these studies will invariably mean making sense of statistics. Many tricks are involved in accurately interpreting statistics. As illustrated in the next chapter, making sense of statistical information does not require sophisticated mathematical knowledge, but rather a "critical eye" that can be developed through experience.

7

Fun figures:
see through the number jumble

Cancer Rates Drop for Second Straight Year: Robust Pipeline of New Medicines Offers Even More Hope.

—Press release headline, January 2007

Pivotal Paper in The Oncologist *from National Cancer Institute Predicts Doubling of Cancer Patients.*

—Press release headline, January 2007

These headlines are great fun to puzzle over, especially because they were published within days of each other. They seem to be completely at odds and probably make many readers want to throw their arms up in dismay, bemoaning how those darned scientists never agree on anything. Yet, a little "secret" can be illuminating. The secret is the difference between the meaning of "rate" and "number." A cancer *rate* is the number of people with cancer within a population of a certain size, usually the number of individuals diagnosed with cancer per 100,000 people. Rates are a handy way of providing data about an illness because rates are independent of the size of the overall population. On the other hand, the *number* of cancer patients does depend on the size of the population. So cancer rates can be holding steady or declining (as the first headline claims) while cancer cases are increasing (as the second headline claims) if the size of the population is increasing. The population of the United

States is indeed increasing. Thus, these headlines are not necessarily at odds. Many secrets like these can help you become more critical of numerical information, whether you are a math whiz or a math-phobe.

Statistics are liberally peppered throughout advertisements, the media, and even advice from acquaintances. On the one hand, statistics help you evaluate the size of a particular risk or benefit. On the other hand, statistics can be misleading. Someone trying to convince you of a particular point of view can easily pick and choose what statistics to present, and how to present them, to make it sound as if something has been scientifically proven. Even when an individual is attempting to present information in an unbiased way, there are many pitfalls of reasoning about statistics that may lead to misinterpretations.

Chapter 3, "Decisions, Decisions," introduced one tricky aspect of reasoning about statistics. Statistics are meaningless without an appropriate context or point of comparison. For example, to evaluate the safety of a particular medical treatment, it is not sufficient to know what percentage of people die after receiving it. The percentage of people who die after being given the treatment must be compared to the percentage who die after other treatments for the same condition and/or the percentage who die when not given any treatment. Putting numbers in context is just one of several essential aspects of evaluating statistical data. The remainder of this chapter reveals the caveats involved in interpreting statistics and explores ways to reason critically about them.

Elucidate hidden confounding factors

Imagine that you want to know which of two hospitals in your area is a better place to have surgery. You compare the surgery survival rates for Hospital 1 and Hospital 2, and find that Hospital 1 has a lower survival rate. Therefore, if you are planning to have surgery, you should try to go to Hospital 2, right? Not so fast. Statistical correlation is not the same as causation. In other words, just because there is a statistical relationship between two factors does not mean that one caused the other. Like the hormone replacement study discussed in Chapter 5, "What Happens If...?," confounding factors could explain the differences observed. Making a sensible comparison of the two hospitals requires additional information. You need to know whether there are any differences in the initial health of patients getting surgery in the two hospitals. If Hospital 1 deals with sicker patients than Hospital 2, the difference in mortality rates between the two hospitals is likely a result of patient differences, rather than differences in the quality of care at the hospitals. For example, does Hospital 1 specialize in geriatric care, or does it have more patients with poor health coverage who only go to see a doctor when an illness is very advanced? You would also need to know what types of surgery are done at each hospital. If one hospital specializes in heart surgery and the other specializes in orthopedic surgery, this could also contribute to the statistical differences observed.

Confounding factors, such as prior health of patients in the hospital scenario, are a serious hindrance to making sense of statistical data. Confounds arise in many other day-to-day uses of statistics as well. For example, data on the salary differences between men and women can be misleading when employment in different sectors is lumped together. Statistics showing that women's average salaries are lower than men's could mean that men earn more than women in the same jobs, or that the fields women favor tend to pay less, or some combination of these two factors. Therefore, the data need to be broken down by field before conclusions can be drawn.

Statistics on flight delays are also misleading if they do not take into consideration what airports an airline flies out of most frequently. It is possible for Ostrich Airlines to have a lower chance of having flight delays than Emu Airlines at every single airport and still have a worse overall flight delay record. For example, this could occur if Ostrich serves San Francisco (which has many delays due to fog) more than Emu, and Emu serves Phoenix (which rarely has inclement weather) more than Ostrich (see Table 7.1).

Table 7.1 Confounded flight delays

	San Francisco flights/week	Delayed	Phoenix flights/week	Delayed	Total Delayed
Ostrich	90	25%=23	10	10%=1	24%
Emu	10	30%=3	90	15%=14	17%

The disentangled data in Table 7.1 show why the "total delayed" statistic can mislead one to think that Emu is the better choice for an on-time flight, even though Ostrich has a lower percentage of delays at both San Francisco and Phoenix than Emu. If flight delay statistics are obtained by airport, or by cause of the delay (weather versus mechanical or other), the statistics are more useful for making a choice of carrier.

Examples like these, where an association or comparison holds true for all of several individual groups (such as flight delays by city) but reverses direction when the groups are combined (total flight delays), are so common that statisticians have given them a name—**Simpson's Paradox**. The possibility that hidden factors are confounding a statistical relationship observed is a major pitfall in making sense of statistical information. Fortunately, as the hospital, employment, and transportation examples show, coming up with factors that may confound a statistical relationship does not require a sophisticated understanding of statistics. It is a matter of thinking outside the box and brainstorming all the reasons a statistical relationship might arise. Why might more surgery patients die at one hospital than another? Why might women earn less than men? Why might one airline have more flight delays than another? Ideally, the person presenting conclusions based on the data would have already checked for hidden factors, but often this does not happen, either because of incompetence or deliberate attempts to mislead. However, once you have identified a potential confounding factor, a little research can reveal whether it is playing a role. For example, a hospital representative should be able to provide information about the number of elective versus emergency surgeries performed.

Determine whether the numbers are statistically significant

If you took an auditorium full of people, randomly separated them into two groups, and surveyed individuals to determine their health history, skills at various sports, artistic abilities, occupations, and so on, the groups' average scores on each factor should be similar. After all, the groups were created at random. However, it is easy enough by chance to end up with one group that contains a few more sports buffs than the other, and one group that contains more artsy types. Health histories would vary as well. In other words, the groups would be similar, but probably not identical on each factor tested. Not only are such variations an issue with populations of humans and other organisms, they arise in all types of measurements. For example, samples of clay that originate from the same lake bed would have similar, but probably not identical, chemical compositions.

Chance variations complicate the interpretation of studies that involve comparing groups. If the average health of one group of patients seems to have improved over the course of treatment with a drug, it is important to know whether that improvement is real or merely a chance variation. Likewise, an archeologist needs to know just how close the chemical composition of clay from a lake bed and the chemical composition of pottery from nearby ruins must be to conclude that the lake bed was the source of the clay used in the pottery. Therefore, to publish a paper in a scientific journal, appropriate statistical tests are required. Researchers use a variety of statistical calculations to decide whether differences between groups are **statistically significant**—real or merely a result of chance. The **level of significance** must also be reported. Results are commonly reported as statistically significant at the 0.05 level. This means that it is 95 percent certain that the observed difference between groups, or sets of samples, is real and could not have arisen by chance. If the results are significant at the 0.01 level, it is 99 percent certain that the apparent differences are real. A related concept is the **margin of error**—the range within which a measurement falls, according to a certain level of confidence. For example, a poll may indicate at 95 percent confidence that 60±5 percent of Americans believe more money should be spent on public transportation. In other words, the pollsters are 95 percent certain that if they could ask every American his or her opinion, somewhere between 55 percent and 65 percent would say that more money should be spent on public transportation.

When it comes to statistical significance, the size of the groups being compared matters. For instance, a poll of ten athletic friends and ten couch potato friends could give you some insight into whether knee problems were associated with participation in sports. However, if five of the athletes and two of the couch potatoes complained of knee pain, would this be good evidence that knee pain is related to participation in sports? Not really, because with such small group sizes, the difference easily could have arisen by chance. On the other hand, if 1,000 athletes and 1,000 couch potatoes were randomly selected and polled, and 500 of the athletes and 200 of the nonathletes had knee pain, this would be much stronger evidence that a correlation existed between knee pain and participation in sports. With such a large sample size, the 50 percent/20 percent statistic could not be due to a few unusual people throwing off the result, as could have been the case with the smaller group.

Of course, even in the large group, the result does not imply that participation in sports causes knee pain. It is equally plausible that the physical characteristics that give people an athletic advantage also ultimately make them susceptible to joint problems, or perhaps athletes just pay more attention to small aches and pains because they are paranoid about being sidelined by injuries. Other kinds of studies would be necessary to get at the relationship between cause and effect. A result that is statistically significant simply means that the difference observed, whatever the underlying cause, is unlikely to have arisen by chance.

Sometimes results presented in a paper are not statistically significant but appear to suggest a trend, which might turn out to be significant in a larger study. The relationships suggested by such trends may merit further examination, but it is risky to draw conclusions based on them. Unfortunately, it happens, and claims are made public without the appropriate caution about statistical significance. Frequently, claims about trends are overturned by later studies, but there may be a considerable gap in time before the next round of studies is completed. In the meantime, the nonstatistically significant result may become folk knowledge that is difficult to overcome when the new results become available. Therefore, when evaluating claims, it is essential to ask whether the study was done with a large enough population for the differences observed to be statistically significant.

Trendy trends

The media loves to make a big deal about trends. Trends make great sound bites:

- Shark attacks on the rise
- Violent crime declining
- Another attack on a foreign tourist
- Safest airlines revealed

Many such "trends" go away as suddenly as they appeared because they were simply temporary fluctuations in data that occur over time.

Determine whether the numbers are statistically meaningful

It is possible for a small effect to be statistically significant. For example, in a trial of a new allergy medication, the reduction in symptoms could turn out to be statistically significant if there were an average difference in the number of sneezes between the drug and placebo groups of one sneeze per day. In other words, in a study involving hundreds or thousands of people, the difference between experimental and control groups does not have to be very large for the statistical tests to conclude that the differences are unlikely to have arisen by chance. As the sneeze example shows, results can be statistically *significant* without being statistically **meaningful**. The allergy drug could be reducing sneezing a little, but what does that mean for a patient's quality of life? An extra sneeze each day is unlikely to make much of a difference. Plus, if the allergy medication has side effects, such as drowsiness, then the patient may have more to lose than to gain from taking the drug.

Making too great a claim based on small differences is a potential pitfall in the allergy example and many other situations. Thus, knowing the size of an effect is as critical as knowing whether the effect is statistically significant. However, that does not mean all small, statistically significant differences should be ignored. If the hypothetical allergy drug caused a meaningful reduction in allergy symptoms but caused a very small elevation in the risk of having a stroke, the drug might not get approval to be marketed. Even the small risk of a life-threatening disease could be considered to outweigh the potential benefits of the drug.

Sometimes graphs, diagrams, and pie charts are used to make numbers seem more meaningful than they are. Diagrams do not have to be drawn to scale, and therefore can be used to exaggerate the difference between two numbers. The axis of a graph can be stretched to make an effect seem larger than it is, or the axis can be compressed to make the effect seem smaller than it is. The number itself may imply a misleading degree of meaningfulness. For example, an advertiser may claim that 63.75 percent of people prefer a new soft drink to the leading brand. Such a precise number makes it seem as though such tests are much more scientific than they are. As discussed previously, because polls always have a margin of error, such precise numbers are meaningless.

Also keep in mind that the number of articles you come across on a particular topic may be completely meaningless with respect to how much that topic can be expected to affect you. Rare disasters draw more media attention than everyday occurrences. For example, statistician Arnold Barnett followed how often the *New York Times* front page ran stories about different modes of death over a two-year period. He reported in the journal *Chance* that there were 138 stories per 1,000 annual deaths from commercial jet crashes and 0.02 stories per 1,000 annual deaths from cancer. The number of stories about these different modes of death could clearly give one a rather distorted sense of risk.

Make sure the statistics apply to the situation

Just because statistics are significant and meaningful does not mean that they apply to the situation or population they are being used to describe. As discussed in the previous chapter, it depends on who or what was the test population, where the data were collected, when they were collected, and under what conditions. Often, pilot studies are done with a small group or in one situation, and if the results are promising, trials are done with other groups, or in other locations, or under other conditions. So it is useful to determine whether the statistics are from a small trial done with a homogeneous population or in a single situation, or from large trials or multiple trials done with heterogeneous populations or in multiple situations.

A noteworthy caveat with human studies is attrition. People drop out of trials for various reasons. They may find that they do not have time to complete all the requirements of the study, or find the commute to the study location too arduous. They may also drop out because they are experiencing side effects of the study treatment. How dropouts are treated in the final analysis is of great concern. Ignoring dropouts who leave the study because of side effects will result in statistics that over-rate the effectiveness of the treatment. If half the people drop out, and 80 percent of the remaining patients show improvement, it would be false to say that the drug worked for 80 percent of people. In fact, it only worked for 40 percent of people in the study. In addition, it is important to determine whether the dropouts were similar to the people who remained in the study, or whether people of a certain age, gender, race, or health status were more likely to experience side effects than others. The characteristics of the dropouts, especially if many people drop out, influence how widely the findings of a study can be applied.

Watch out for selection bias

Opinion polls and surveys are particularly vulnerable to statistical mishaps and deliberate trickery. The outcome of a survey can be influenced in two important ways. The first is selection bias. It takes a considerable amount of work to conduct a survey to get responses from a reasonably random group of people. For example, surveys conducted outside a shopping mall, concert, or sports arena may not be balanced in terms of people's income levels, race, or gender. Also, people who feel strongly about the topic of the survey are more likely to complete it than people who do not. So stakeholders who want to bias their survey can cleverly select who answers it, and even the most well-meaning pollster may accidentally bias a survey by failing to get a representative sample.

The second way to bias a survey is to manipulate the wording of the questions, or the way the survey is conducted. For example, significantly more people respond in favor of "Should more tax dollars be used to help the poor?" than respond in favor of "Should more tax dollars be used for welfare?" Also, when people are asked about controversial issues, it is common for them to lie to an interviewer to appear kinder and more open-minded. For example, they may say they will vote for increasing property taxes to support schools, but fail to do so when they go to the polls. They may also lie to better conform to social norms if they do not think their responses will truly be kept anonymous, or if they feel uncomfortable being pressured to reveal personal information to an interviewer.

Selection bias lives on in infamy

What was arguably the all-time greatest example of selection bias resulted in the embarrassing 1948 *Chicago Tribune* headline "Dewey defeats Truman." In reality, Harry Truman trounced his opponent. All the major political polls at the time had predicted Thomas Dewey would be elected president. The *Chicago Tribune* went to press before the election results were in, its editors confident that the polls would be correct. The statisticians were wrong for two reasons. First, they stopped polling too far in advance of the election, and Truman was especially successful at energizing people in the final days before the election. Second, the telephone polls conducted tended to favor Dewey because in 1948, telephones were generally limited to wealthier households, and

Dewey was mainly popular among elite voters. The selection bias that resulted in the infamous *Chicago Tribune* headline was accidental, but it shows the danger and potential power—for a stakeholder wanting to influence hearts and minds by encouraging others to hop on the bandwagon—of selection bias.

Ask whether a statistical change reflects reality or the way the data were collected

Between 1994 and 2004, the number of children in the U.S. public schools classified as having autism and related health problems, collectively known as autism spectrum disorders, increased more than 800 percent. Autism spectrum disorders (ASDs) cost the U.S. economy more than $35 billion per year. More children are diagnosed with ASDs than with cancer, diabetes, and AIDS combined. The cause of this remarkably sudden ASD epidemic? There are controversial opinions for the cause, but no proven reasons. It occurred over too short a time to be purely genetic, although a number of genes have been implicated in autism. So researchers are looking for environmental factors, such as chemicals or microbes, that might be harming children who are genetically susceptible to ASDs. In other words, individuals could have genetic differences that put some of them at risk of getting ASDs if they are exposed to certain environmental factors. Perhaps a growing number of children are being exposed to those environmental factors, resulting in a growing number of children diagnosed with ASDs.

Another explanation is possible. Maybe there is no ASD epidemic at all. On the surface, this may seem like a silly thing to say. Such large increases in ASD diagnoses must be statistically significant and meaningful. Indeed they are, but only if the increases truly reflect an increase in the number of people with the disorder, as opposed to a new way of counting people with the disorder. Back in the "good old days" when—as our parents or grandparents like to tell us—kids had to walk three miles to school (uphill in both directions), no one talked about autism. A child who had difficulty communicating and engaging in social activities, the hallmark of ASDs, would simply have been called a loner or antisocial. If the condition were severe enough, the child would probably have been labeled mentally retarded. In our more medically savvy (and overanxious) society, parents would be more likely to haul their little loner off to a doctor. The more aware parents and doctors are about ASDs, the more children are likely to be (correctly or incorrectly) diagnosed with these disorders. One doctor even confided to an autism researcher that if a child's symptoms were borderline, he would "squeeze" out an autism diagnosis if he could. His behavior was not nefarious. He knew that there were more services for children diagnosed with autism than with other types of learning disabilities, so he was trying to help the children's parents. Given these caveats, most autism researchers believe that there has been an increase in the number of children with ASDs, but that it is not nearly as large as the statistics suggest.

Medical diagnoses are not completely objective. Diseases fall in and out of fashion. The symptoms of different diseases are often similar. Heightened awareness about a disease on the part of a doctor or patient makes it more likely a patient will be diagnosed with that disease. Just giving something a name guarantees that more people will be diagnosed with it. Behaviors that used to be considered within the range of normal, such as hyperactivity and moodiness, are increasingly labeled and treated as illnesses, such as attention deficit disorder or bipolar disorder. Also, invasive tests as well as full-body scans and brain scans are increasingly prevalent. These tests are bound to turn up things that would never have been noticed otherwise. For example, a small benign tumor that shows up on a scan of a person's abdomen might never have caused any health problems or otherwise have been detected. Future studies of medical trends over time will reveal a dramatic increase in tumor diagnoses that corresponds to when these new technologies were introduced. It is quite likely that at some point, someone will see that increase, fail to link it with the introduction of full-body scans, and speculate about the chemicals in our environment that suddenly caused people to start sprouting tumors all over the place.

Medicine is not the only field in which changes in data collection procedures can make it seem as if reality has changed when it has not. Another example is pollution monitoring. As more sensitive tests become available, it is possible to detect pollutants in the air or water that were previously undetectable. Therefore, when interpreting trends over time, it is important to determine whether there have been any changes in the procedures or tools used to collect data that could contribute to the statistical changes observed.

Putting it all together

The scientific issues that impact our daily lives, as well as scientific problems in general, virtually always have something to do with cause and effect, either determining the cause of an observation or determining how to cause a desired result. As illustrated by the examples in Chapters 5 and 6, and in this chapter, it is easy to get the impression that two things are causally linked when the link between them is indirect or they are not linked at all. Questions that can be used to evaluate the purported relationship between cause and effect are listed in the following sidebar.

Checklist to determine the relationship between alleged cause and outcome

- What could be other possible causes of an observation? Can they be ruled out?
- If not, could they act in concert with the alleged cause, or could they be part of a chain of events with the alleged cause?
- Is there a plausible mechanism linking the alleged cause and outcome?
- Do multiple studies link the alleged cause and outcome? Is the relationship consistent across studies?
- Has the relationship held up across different individuals, locations, and conditions, and over time? If not, is there a logical reason that the relationship does not exist in all cases?
- Are the data being used to describe the relationship statistically significant, meaningful, free of confounding factors, and representative of reality rather than some quirk in the way the data were collected?
- Can the statistics be legitimately applied to the situation at hand?

Several criteria must be met before it is reasonable to conclude that an alleged cause really did lead to the observed outcome. Other possible causes must be examined and systematically ruled out. If they cannot be ruled out, the possibility that there are multiple causes, or a chain of causes and effects, should be explored. The alleged cause must precede the effect observed, and the alleged cause should be feasible. Ideally, there should be a plausible mechanism to explain the relationship between cause and effect. The cause and effect relationship should hold true in multiple studies, and across multiple individuals and situations, unless there is a valid reason for the relationship to break down under certain circumstances. The data being used to prove the existence of the causal relationship and indicate its strength must be statistically significant and meaningful. They cannot be influenced by hidden factors or be an artifact of the way the data were collected. Finally, statistics only apply to the same circumstances as those under which they were collected. Attrition of subjects from experimental studies and other limitations of experimental design can affect how widely the statistics apply.

The preceding chapters introduced the big picture and the finer points of evaluating claims and evidence. We also saw how different stakeholders interpret information in subjective ways. Now armed with an understanding of how science progresses, the types of tradeoffs that arise in science-based issues, how to put things in context, and the caveats of interpreting scientific evidence, we can explore the decision-making of a group of stakeholders who deserve special attention—those who make policy about scientific issues. Policy makers, including politicians, judges, and people who work at regulatory agencies—such as the Environmental Protection Agency, the Food and Drug Administration, and the Department of Agriculture in the United States, and similar agencies in other countries—have a profound influence on how we live. They influence how science is done and what actions are taken on the basis of, sometimes inadequate, scientific knowledge. Even the best decisions—ones that truly result from an examination of the big picture and the fine points of claims and evidence—have a degree of subjectivity associated with them because values come into play when making tradeoffs. The next chapter explores the many societal factors that influence policy decisions.

8

Society's say: discern the relationships between science and policy

At a zoo, visitors may witness a great beast pacing behind the bars of its cage. They may observe and admire the creature, its exquisite bone structure, magnificent coat, and the fiery determination of its expression. Perhaps the zookeepers have installed a sign describing the creature's physiology and a unique anatomical adaptation it has. Passersby may read the information with fascination, but no matter how long they spend in front of that cage, they will never truly understand the beast. True understanding can only come from seeing the creature in its natural surroundings, knowing where it fits in the web of life, what features of the physical environment are crucial for it to survive and thrive, and, in turn, the ways in which its presence affects its environment.

What is true of the mysterious beast in the zoo is also true of science. To fully understand science, it must be considered within the society in which it functions. Science is not conducted in a vacuum. It is embedded within a social fabric, and just as a flesh-and-blood beast influences and is influenced by its environment in a reciprocal manner, so too do science and society influence one another reciprocally. Society, through ethical and economic constraints, exerts a powerful influence on what science gets done. At the same time, the results of science and the products resulting from applications of basic science have profound, and some-times unexpected, impacts on every human being on earth. Therefore, to make sense of science-related issues, it is critical to recognize the bidi-rectional relationship between science and society and to identify the influences on policy decisions. This chapter examines how policies influence science and how policies are derived from science.

Morals and money—influences on the progress of science

From Mary Shelley's *Frankenstein* to Michael Crichton's *Jurassic Park*, fiction writers have long crafted compelling narratives about mad scientists and science run amuck. Real-life examples in which scientists have crossed a clear line between right and wrong do exist, but today the ethical decisions facing real scientists and those who make decisions about science are often much thornier than those depicted in fictional accounts.

Coercion and lies

In 1932 in Tuskegee, Alabama, 600 African American men were enrolled in what would become the most infamous medical research study in American history. The men, who were poor sharecroppers, were promised free medical treatment, transportation to and from the clinic, hot meals, and burial insurance. They were told that they had "bad blood," but the actual diagnosis, for 399 of the men (the rest served as controls), was syphilis. When the study began, the available syphilis remedies were toxic and not very effective. Part of the rationale for the study, in addition to tracking the natural progression of the disease, was to determine whether patients were better off without these toxic treatments. However, penicillin became available as an effective treatment for syphilis in 1947, and the Tuskegee Syphilis Study continued until 1972, but the infected men were never treated with penicillin. Instead, the researchers, intent on studying the natural progression of the disease, lied to and coerced the men to prevent them from seeking treatment. By the end of the study, 128 of the men had died of syphilis or related complications, 40 of their wives had been infected, and 19 of their children were born with congenital syphilis. The study ended 40 years after it began when a leak to the press resulted in public outcry.

Ethics and oversight

Many of the oversights and regulations now in place in the United States to protect people who participate in medical research were introduced as a direct result of the fallout over the Tuskegee Syphilis Study. Institutions that perform human studies in medicine and psychology, including clinical trials of new drugs, must have Institutional Review Boards (IRBs)—independent ethical oversight committees—to protect the rights and welfare of research subjects. To conduct a study involving humans, researchers must submit a protocol to their institution's IRB detailing the scientific merits of the proposed study, the procedures in place to provide potential subjects with information that will enable them to give their fully informed consent to participate in the study, and the procedures that will maximize the safety of those enrolled in the study. Extra attention is given to trials that involve individuals who are particularly vulnerable, or may not have the capacity to give their full informed consent, such as children, prisoners, the elderly, and people with mental illness or mental handicaps.

Regulations to protect laboratory animals and human embryos have also constrained medical research. However, not all ethical considerations create new limitations. Some have the opposite effect. For example, successful efforts to make it illegal to discriminate against people on the basis of genetic information could make people more likely to get a genetic test or participate in research that involves genetic testing. Otherwise, people may avoid genetic tests, fearing that if they test positive for a gene that could predispose them to develop a certain disease they could lose out on health insurance or employment opportunities. Medicine is not the only area of science in which new ethical considerations have influenced what scientific research gets done and how it is accomplished. Norms are also shifting in archeology. Professional organizations of archeologists have become increasingly culturally sensitive to indigenous people who view relics as sacred and consider human remains to be their ancestors, even if the remains are thousands of years old. Similarly, researchers who study nature-derived compounds for use in medications, nutritional supplements, cosmetics, or industrial processes are now less likely to exploit the knowledge of indigenous people without giving them a share of any profits from commercialization of what was originally their discovery.

Ethics from the inside

Changing social norms is just one reason that new regulations may be put in place to keep scientific research in check. Another reason is that scientific advances may introduce ethical dilemmas or safety concerns that were previously entirely hypothetical, or completely unenvisioned. The scientific advances that made it possible to manipulate the genes of an organism, and even swap DNA between organisms as different as a bacterium and a human, have opened a bigger can of worms than perhaps any other scientific advance. When recombinant DNA technology—the ability to combine DNA from different organisms—first became a reality, the research was temporarily halted so that safety issues could be evaluated. However, it was not public outcry that led to the halting of the research, it was caution and concern on the part of the scientists themselves. A group of leading researchers sent a letter to the president of the U.S. National Academy of Sciences requesting that a committee be appointed to study the safety ramifications of the new technology. The committee recommended a moratorium on it until an international conference could be convened to come up with a workable solution.

That now famous conference was held at the Asilomar Conference Center in California in 1975. It brought together more than 100 biologists, along with lawyers and physicians, to establish voluntary guidelines for experiments involving recombinant DNA technology. Of primary concern was the possibility that engineered organisms (specifically bacteria and viruses) could escape the laboratory and endanger the health of humans or the environment. Therefore, the guidelines focused on preventing escape, and minimizing the spread of the engineered organisms in the case of escape, by applying precautionary measures appropriate for the level of risk involved in a particular experiment. These measures included physical containment through the use of specific laboratory procedures and equipment, and biological containment through the use of bacteria and viruses that could not survive outside the laboratory. After the Asilomar Conference, discussions about the research continued and also involved philosophers, theologians, and other nonscientists. Over time the fears engendered by this type of research have diminished. We have genetically engineered crops, bacteria engineered for the industrial-scale production of drugs to treat human diseases, bacteria engineered to help clean up oil spills, and a whole new industry, the biotechnology industry. Although ethical concerns remain about certain uses of recombinant DNA technology, such as the possibility of engineering human embryos, the scientific community's response to the technology when it first emerged set a precedent for how to deal with scientific advances considered to have significant potential risks. Specifically, guidelines should be developed on the basis of discussions among individuals with different expertise, including scientists and nonscientists.

Unintended consequences

Clearly ethical considerations in science are critical. The health and well-being of the general public, the environment, and human and animal research subjects must be protected even when doing so is detrimental to scientific progress. However, some regulations imposed in response to ethical considerations have unintended consequences and fail to protect those they are intended to protect. An example is former President George W. Bush's strange constraint on stem cell research. While he was in office, federal funding could not be used for research on any human embryonic stem cell lines created after August 9, 2001. His rationale was that this would protect human embryos from being sacrificed for scientific research, but would not hinder progress toward the development of stem cell therapies. The scientific community argued, to no avail, that the older stem cell lines had defects—such as contamination with animal cells that were added to the culture medium to help keep the human stem cells alive—that made them unsuitable for use in stem cells therapies. At the same time, Bush's decision failed to protect human embryos, since private research funding could still be used to make and use new stem cell lines. The regulations pushed some stem cell researchers to move to countries with fewer restrictions on stem cell research. Those who stayed in the United States had to make sure that equipment purchased with federal grant funds was not being used for research on new stem cell lines. That meant researchers had to set up complex accounting procedures if their labs received private and federal research dollars and did research on old and new stem cell lines.

Bush's compromise frustrated the scientific community, but it probably did not inflict extra harm on the human embryos it was meant to protect. In contrast, the additional effort it takes to gain Institutional Review Board approval to conduct clinical trials of drugs on children may cause children unintended harm. Physicians and psychiatrists will still prescribe the drugs for children "off label"—that is, without the drugs having been tested on children in clinical trials. The problem is that children are not mini adults. Their metabolisms work differently. Their bodies may break down drugs more quickly or more slowly than adults. They may respond to drugs completely differently than adults. Therefore, when a child is prescribed a drug that has not been tested in clinical trials involving children, that child is a guinea pig. Clinical trials are set up to monitor adverse reactions, fine-tune doses, and objectively measure improvement. On the other hand, doctors prescribing drugs to individual patients may not communicate with other doctors doing the same. If patients' adverse reactions are not life threatening, they may never be carefully reviewed by the research community, and despite good intentions on the part of their doctors, many more children may end up receiving substandard care than would have been involved in clinical trials had they been conducted. In response to this problem, regulatory agencies in the United States and Europe have recently implemented programs to encourage drug companies to conduct appropriate clinical trials with children, and develop drugs designed specifically for children.

Ethics is not the only factor that influences what science gets done and how it is accomplished. The availability of money, from philanthropists, governments, or industry, also plays an enormous role. No matter how much a society supports scientific research, the pot of research dollars will always be limited, and the number of research questions and problems to be solved unlimited. Societies must therefore set priorities on what research should be funded according to the pressing issues of the day. Geographical surveys and expeditions were research priorities early in the history of many nations. Agriculture was another early research priority. Now concerns about global climate change and rising oil prices have increased the funding of research into alternative sources of energy. Of course, old problems do not necessarily go away, and new problems may not really be new. The energy crisis of the 1970s also stimulated many nations to fund research on alternative energy. For example, the military regime in power in Brazil at the time wanted to reduce dependence on foreign oil, so it subsidized the production of ethanol from sugarcane. The subsidies helped the industry make tremendous advances, and Brazilian sugarcane ethanol is now cost competitive with gasoline on world markets. Although the issues facing society guide the allocation of research funding, resources are not distributed in a strictly rational manner. Pride, fear, and power all influence how research funding is allocated. In addition, the source of funding can influence the results and interpretation of the results of research studies.

Pride of nations

On October 4, 1957, the Soviet Union launched Sputnik, a 184-pound basketball-sized satellite. It was an act that struck fear into the hearts of the American people. The satellite itself was no threat. It merely circled the earth every hour and a half, emitting radio signals as it whizzed past at 18,000 miles per hour. Three months after launch, it burned up in the atmosphere. Still, the demise of the little satellite was no consolation. Americans had been confident of their technological might, yet the Russians had managed to beat them in this extremely important endeavor. The damage to America's national pride meant that Sputnik's ghost influenced policy decisions in the United States for years, even decades, after hoards of amateur radio enthusiasts came out to track the beeping ball in the sky. In the wake of Sputnik, overall federal research expenditures grew significantly, and The National Defense Education Act was passed to provide more funds for mathematics and science education in the interest of national security. The National Aeronautics and Space Administration (NASA) was created in 1958, and in 1961, in an effort to restore national prestige, President Kennedy promised the American people that they would be the first to make it to the moon. At the peak of the race to the moon, NASA's research and development budget grew to one-third of the total federal research and development budget. The post-Sputnik boost to U.S. science reflected a public and political consensus about the importance of science and technology. Much research, especially in the physical sciences, could be demonstrated to be related to Cold War concerns in one way or another. Scientists growing up during the post-Sputnik era often point to Sputnik as having planted the seed that grew into their own interest in science. Sputnik made science cool and patriotic.

This snapshot from the Cold War clearly illustrates that national pride can influence how science is funded and what science gets done. The influence of national pride on science is not limited to the Cold War, or to the United States and Russia. As China has emerged as an economic superpower, it has also invested in manned space flight and announced plans to go to the moon. National pride and national defense interests are intertwined, but they are not one and the same. To be sure, national defense interests such as the development of nuclear weapons by several countries, including India and Pakistan, have a significant element of pride associated with them and helping drive them. But the tremendous amount of money that it costs to send humans into space cannot be justi-fied on the basis of national security. In fact, NASA's budget fell sharply once the race to the moon had been won, although the Cold War showed no signs of coming to an end. Science in the interest of national pride is not necessarily a bad thing, especially when it gives science a higher pro-file and inspires young people to consider careers in the sciences. But it is important to recognize that the money for expensive, grand vision proj-ects must come from somewhere, and other very good projects may be shortchanged as a result. NASA's struggle to find funds for a mission to the Hubble Space Telescope to complete repairs needed to extend the telescope's life, while the agency simultaneously geared up to respond to President Bush's vision to return to the moon and send humans to Mars, illustrates this difficult balancing act.

Fear of the grim reaper

The era of big physics ended when the Soviet Union collapsed, and for a while Americans lost their fear of getting left behind. At the same time, those born in the heady days after the Iron Curtain descended were beginning to fear a new, more personal enemy. Aging. The baby boomers' fear of getting old and infirm ushered in a new era—the era of big biology. The sequencing of the human genome, which began in 1990 and took more than a decade, involved hundreds of researchers and cost nearly $3 billion. It was biology's man-on-the-moon moment in the way it captured the public's attention. But a wide gulf exists between coming up with a list of DNA sequence information that would fill 200 telephone books and putting that information to use in curing and preventing dis-ease. Therefore, the era of big biology is not likely to end anytime soon, especially while the U.S. population continues to age.

Most of the medical research paid for by U.S. taxpayers is funded by the National Institutes of Health (NIH), which has seen its budget grow dramatically over the years, doubling between 1998 and 2003. Few would argue that funding research programs aimed at ending human suf-fering is a poor use of taxpayers' money. On the contrary, people make substantial voluntary donations to private foundations and come out *en masse* to participate in marathons, walk-a-thons, and other events to raise money to fund disease research. Still, even with the support of the public, and the tens of billions of dollars available for disease research, tough choices must be made about how to allocate research funds among the many, many illnesses that plague humankind. Faced with these tough choices, is there a clear rationale used by public agencies to divvy up the available research dollars? A simple way to distribute the funds would be based on how many people die of a particular disease. The calculation is straightforward. First, take the total dollar amount available for health research and divide it by the number of people who died of any illness in the previous year. That yields the dollar amount available for research per human life lost. Second, to determine the size of the pot of funds that should be available for each disease, multiply the number of people who died of that disease in the previous year by the dollar amount available per life lost.

A cursory look at the top ten causes of death in the United States and the NIH funding allocated to the corresponding diseases, listed in Table 8.1, makes it clear that loss of life is not the only factor playing a role in funding decisions. Stroke and chronic lung disease—more technically known as chronic obstructive pulmonary disease—the third and fourth most common causes of death respectively, are dramatically under-funded compared to the sixth through ninth most common causes of death. One possible explanation for the discrepancy is that Americans' tax dollars are allocated to health research in a more altruistic manner—that is, the rest of the world is taken into consideration. However, the explanation is incorrect. Stroke and chronic lung disease are among the top killers worldwide, but Alzheimer's disease is not. In middle and lower income countries, infectious diseases and complications of pregnancy and childbirth claim many more lives.

Another puzzling observation about the allocation of health funding for the top ten causes of death in the United States is that research on infectious diseases (influenza, pneumonia, and septicemia—an inflam-matory state throughout the body that is caused by infection) is being shortchanged relative to research on noninfectious diseases. It is difficult to think of a logical argument to shortchange infectious disease research. On the contrary, there are two good arguments in favor of allocating extra public funds to research on infectious diseases. First, infectious diseases are not predictable. New strains of bacteria and viruses are always emerging, and any new strain has the potential to cause a pan-demic. Second, industry is less likely to invest in research on antibiotics and antiviral medicines than in research on medicines for chronic diseases, which are considerably more profitable. With the exception of antiviral medications for HIV/AIDS, most antibiotics and antivirals are taken by patients for relatively short periods of time. Cash cows such as cholesterol medicines—some of which rank among the greatest selling drugs of all time—must be taken every day for years, even decades. Furthermore, since bacteria and viruses are always evolving, it is not unusual for these medicines to become obsolete relatively quickly. Because private companies are insufficiently motivated to find new methods to combat infectious agents, it would make sense for public agencies to pick up the slack.

TABLE 8.1   Top killers and funding decisions

Cause of death	Number of deaths[°] (U.S. 2004)	NIH funding[°°] (U.S. 2005)
1. Heart disease	652,486	$2,087 million
2. Cancer	553,888	$5,639 million
3. Stroke	150,074	$342 million
4. Chronic lung disease	121,987	$63 million
5. Accidents	112,012	N/A
6. Diabetes	73,138	$1,055 million
7. Alzheimer's disease	65,965	$656 million
8. Influenza/pneumonia	59,664	$317 million
9. Kidney disease	42,480	$427 million
10. Septicemia	33,373	$42 million

[°]From the Centers for Disease Control (www.cdc.gov).
[°°]From the National Institutes of Health (www.nih.gov).

Fear may be a significant factor in the funding of health research, just as fear played a role in the allocation of resources during the Cold War. There was a time that many scientists and members of the public truly believed humankind was beating infectious diseases, and that bacterial diseases at least would soon be a thing of the past. The emergence of antibiotic resistant bacteria certainly makes headlines and worries members of the public, but perhaps there remains a sense that we already have the tools to beat back the microbes. Fear could also explain why Alzheimer's disease, which kills less than half as many people as are killed by strokes, gets nearly twice as much funding. A disease that slowly robs people of their mental faculties is a lot scarier than one that takes you out quickly. Of course, strokes can also rob people of their mental faculties, but Alzheimer's seems more horrific because a diagnosis of Alzheimer's means a gradual, irreversible decline, while there is hope of recovery for many stroke survivors.

Power of the people

Since cancer affects young and old, athletes and couch potatoes alike, it is not surprising that it attracts more research funding than any other disease. Another reason is that cancer is not a single disease, but more than 100 different diseases. That makes it a tough nut to crack. So it is logical to dedicate more research dollars to cancer than would be warranted based on mortality data. However, even within cancer research, factors other than the number of deaths influence what research gets funded (see Table 8.2). For example, breast cancer and prostate cancer are much better funded than would be expected according to how many lives they take. The funding does not correspond to years of life lost either. Prostate cancer kills at a later age than the other cancers listed, but it receives the second highest amount of funding. The discrepancy can be partly explained by how many people are diagnosed with each type of cancer (see Table 8.3). There are more new cases of prostate and breast cancer than other types of cancer. However, neither deaths nor number of diagnoses can explain why pancreatic cancer research gets less funding than ovarian cancer research. Data on deaths and diagnoses also does not explain why lung cancer research gets less than half as much funding as breast cancer research. Prejudice relating to the connection between smoking and lung cancer (although many lung cancer victims never smoked) may explain the relatively low funding for research on lung cancer, but it cannot explain the relatively low funding for research on pancreatic cancer. Levels of fear about the diseases cannot explain the discrepancy either, since the later stages of any cancer are equally devastating. Therefore, other forces must play a role.

TABLE 8.2   Cancer deaths and funding decisions

Type of cancer	Estimated deaths (U.S. 2006)°	Median age at death°°	NCI funding (U.S 2006)°°
Lung	162,460	71	$265 million
Colon and Rectum	55,170	75	$252 million
Breast	41,430	69	$557 million
Pancreas	32,300	74	$74 million
Prostate	27,350	80	$309 million
Ovary	15,310	71	$95 million

TABLE 8.3   New cancer diagnoses

Type of cancer	Estimated cases (U.S. 2006)°	Difference between median age at diagnosis and at death°°
Lung	174,470	1
Colon and Rectum	106,680	4
Breast	214, 640	8
Pancreas	33,730	2
Prostate	234,460	12
Ovary	20,180	8

°From CA: A Cancer Journal for Clinicians (2006), Volume 56, pp. 106-130.
°°From the National Cancer Institute (www.cancer.gov).

Power plays a significant role in how research funds are allocated among different diseases, and patient advocacy groups wield that power. For cancer alone, there are more than 1,000 different advocacy groups. The lobbying efforts of breast cancer and prostate cancer advocacy groups have been especially successful. Why do certain cancer advocacy groups have louder voices than others? One factor seems to be a bias in favor of less lethal diseases. The majority of people diagnosed with breast cancer or prostate cancer survive, and even those who succumb to the disease live for many years after they have been diagnosed. In contrast, lung cancer and pancreatic cancer are nearly always fatal, and the time between diagnosis and death is very short. Ovarian cancer is usually fatal, but it does not kill as quickly. The longer patients survive after being diagnosed with a disease, the more time they have to become advocates for that disease, and the more time there is for their struggle to motivate friends and family to become advocates on their behalf.

In direct contrast with the power of patient advocacy groups in cancer research are the many fewer voices, and corresponding lack of power, advocating for research on diseases that primarily affect people in developing nations. For example, malaria kills more than one million people each year and sickens millions more. The NIH budget for malaria is $100 million per year, about the same as its budget for ovarian cancer, which affects a tiny fraction of as many people. Diseases of the developing world also do not attract private research funding because companies do not want to spend big bucks to develop drugs for people who cannot afford them. This brutal reality has stimulated the U.S. Food and Drug Administration to offer incentives for companies to develop treatments for so-called neglected diseases, such as malaria, dengue fever, and hookworm. A company that develops a treatment for a neglected disease is granted a voucher that guarantees fast-track review of another drug of its choosing—presumably a potential blockbuster aimed at treating a disease that afflicts people who can pay for it.

Ethical considerations and available research funding are not the only nonscientific influences on science; another factor is the patenting of engineered organisms, genes, and research techniques. The opportunity to obtain a patent may stimulate innovation, but patents can also be roadblocks when scientists must gain permissions and pay fees to work with the information they need. Political agendas are another external influence on science, and although they were discussed earlier, it is important to note that their influence is not purely financial. Simply the excitement generated by putting an issue in the limelight can encourage more researchers to take an interest in it. The following quotation nicely summarizes the role of societal influences on what science gets done.

We should explain how research priorities are set, because it is not nature whispering into the ears of researchers, but an intricate mixture of opportunities and incentives, of prior investments and of strategic planning mixed with subversive contingencies.[1]

[1] Helga Nowotny, *Science*, 308, 1117. May 20, 2005.

Every citizen needs to know that society exerts a powerful influence on how research priorities are set because it means that each of us can play a role in these decisions. Since different politicians and political parties have different agendas, voting is one way we influence the setting of research priorities. We can also lobby our politicians, who ultimately answer to their constituents, or we can become members of groups that engage in such lobbying efforts. To use our voices wisely, we need to remember that payoffs of research often come from unexpected sources, so we cannot afford to be shortsighted. A breakthrough that leads to a new treatment for a disease may come from research on a different disease, or basic scientific research aimed at understanding normal processes in a cell. Using our voices wisely also entails educating ourselves on all sides of an issue, and not jumping to conclusions on the basis of incomplete information, even if the information triggers an emotional reaction. That may mean finding a middle ground when different groups of researchers, funded by different sources, come to contradictory conclusions.

Follow the money

The flow of research dollars determines not only what research gets done, but also how it gets done. The influence of the source of funding on how science gets done can result in industry-funded and public-funded scientists coming to different conclusions and challenging one another's claims. Such differences can arise without any deliberate falsification of data, especially when the effects being observed are relatively subtle. Two bodies of literature, one regarding the health effects of an ingredient found in some plastics, and the other regarding the possibility that antidepressant medications can increase suicide risk, illustrate these differences and some of the factors that give rise to them.

Poisons in plastics?

The chemical bisphenol A (BPA) is found in 95 percent of urine samples from people in the United States, according to the Centers for Disease Control and Prevention. BPA is in the main ingredient in polycarbonate plastics, which are used to make shatter-resistant baby bottles and sports bottles. BPA is also used in some dental sealants and the lacquers used to coat the inside of metal food cans, bottle tops, and water pipes. For most people, the main route of exposure to BPA is through the diet, but because BPA has been produced and used in such large quantities (more than six billion pounds globally each year as of 2007), it is widespread in the environment. In high doses, BPA is toxic to laboratory animals, a finding that is well established and neither controversial nor worrisome. After all, many vitamins and minerals are lethal in large doses. The controversy is over whether BPA is harmful in low doses, similar to those that people are exposed to in daily life.

Studies in which low doses of BPA were administered to animals or isolated cells indicate that BPA may mimic the effects of estrogen. However, the outcomes of the studies are highly variable. Some reveal no adverse effects; others conclude that BPA may cause obesity, cancer, or both, and other studies report milder effects. Studies' outcomes depend on the source of the funds used to complete them. A review of BPA studies published in the August 2005 issue of the journal *Environmental Health Perspectives* found that 90 percent of government-funded studies reported significant health effects of low doses of BPA, but none of the industry-funded studies did. It would be easy to conclude that the industry-funded scientists are all biased, whereas government-funded scientists are not, but it is not necessarily so clear-cut. Government-funded researchers could be biased by the need to secure research funds. If it looked like there was nothing to the BPA story, funds dedicated to investigating it would dry up.

BPA studies by both groups of researchers were criticized by a panel of independent experts at the National Toxicology Program (NTP) of the U.S. National Institutes of Health. The NTP panel identified three major flaws in the studies. First, studies often included too few animals to produce statistically significant results. Second, many studies failed to account for the fact that the response to BPA is more similar for animals from the same litter than for animals from different litters. Third, many studies omitted a positive control. Usually a control, as discussed in Chapter 5, "What Happens If...?," is a sham treatment meant to guard against the placebo effect. A positive control is the opposite. It is a treatment with something that is known to produce an effect (in this case, a known estrogen), and is used to prove that the experiment is working. Otherwise, when the outcome of a study is that the animals showed no response to BPA, it is impossible to know whether that means BPA has no effects, or that there was a flaw in the experimental design. For example, the *Environmental Health Perspectives* article argued that the industry studies had used a strain of rats that is rather insensitive to estrogen. Another potential confound is that rodent feed sometimes contains plant-based estrogens that could mask the effects of BPA.

In April 2008, after comparing the results of 500 BPA studies and considering the issues of experimental design, the NTP panel published a draft report on the effects of low doses of BPA. The panelists concluded that BPA exposure in adults was unlikely to cause reproductive problems, and that BPA exposure during pregnancy was unlikely to cause any major birth defects or developmental problems. However, they had some concern that exposure to BPA in fetuses, infants, and children could cause neural and behavioral changes, affect the prostate gland and mammary glands, and lead to an earlier age of puberty in females. They also concluded that the existing data were insufficient to determine whether these changes could increase the risk of cancer later in life. Ironically, industry representatives claimed that the NTP panel's report vindicated BPA, while others used the report to conclude that BPA should be eliminated from food and beverage containers.

Depressing antidepressants?

Starting in 2003, regulatory agencies in the United Kingdom, Canada, the United States, and elsewhere issued warnings that newer antidepressants (particularly selective serotonin reuptake inhibitors, or SSRIs) could increase the risk of suicide in children and adolescents. It is always a matter of concern when serious side effects of a medication come to light after the medication has been approved, but it is particularly disturbing when the new "side effect" is something the medication was meant to alleviate in the first place. Not surprisingly, the pharmaceutical industry denied that there was any connection between the use of antidepressants and suicide. Others have criticized the industry for failing to publish the results of trials with negative or questionable results, thereby creating a bias in the published literature that makes antidepressants appear more effective than they are.

As with the research on BPA, the research on how children respond to antidepressants is fraught with complexities. First, studies do not show that there are more suicides among children on antidepressants than among those given a placebo. The overall number of suicides in the studies is too low to be statistically significant, in part because it is considered unethical to give a placebo to individuals at high risk of suicide, so they are usually excluded from placebo-controlled studies of antidepressants. Instead, the warnings of the regulatory agencies have been based on reports of self-harm behaviors and suicidal thoughts. These reports suggest antidepressants may make some youngsters more impulsive, and therefore more suicidal, when they first go on the drug and before its antidepressant action kicks in. Alternatively, since most antidepressants have only been tested in adults and are being prescribed for children "off label," some doctors fear that the problem may be due to a failure to prescribe the correct dose. If the dose is too high, it may make the serotonin receptors less sensitive—the opposite of what the drugs are meant to do—and worsen depression. Furthermore, the responses may be different for different antidepressants, and not all children seem to be affected the same way.

The general consensus among doctors and researchers is that antidepressants could cause some children, possibly those with bipolar disorder rather than straight depression, to have more suicidal thoughts. Until it is determined who is at risk, the warnings of the regulatory agencies seem like a reasonable precaution. Unfortunately, the warnings have had unintended consequences. A study published in the April 8, 2008, *Canadian Medical Association Journal* (*CMAJ*) found that after the warnings were issued, fewer children and adolescents sought treatment for depression, fewer were prescribed antidepressants, and the rate of suicide among children and adolescents increased. Prescriptions of antidepressants for young adults also declined, even though young adults were not the target of the warnings. Furthermore, prescriptions of SSRIs to children, adolescents, and young adults with anxiety disorders declined following the warnings. Although SSRIs are used to treat both depression and anxiety disorders, the warnings were not intended to apply to patients with anxiety disorders. The *CMAJ* study illustrates that regulatory agencies need to take potential public reaction into consideration when making policy decisions, and take steps to educate the public when overreaction to a decision could be harmful.

The BPA and SSRI controversies make it clear that the source of funding can influence the results of research studies. The influence may be deliberate or inadvertent, but for complex issues, it is rarely the case that one camp's science is completely distorted, while the other camp's science is beyond reproach. Since these controversies often involve hundreds of studies, it is not realistic for one person to sort through and evaluate all of them. For this reason, the findings of independent panels of experts are helpful. The independent review panels (NTP and FDA) found that neither BPA nor SSRIs are as harmless as the Pollyannas would lead us to believe, nor as dangerous as the Chicken Littles claim. As a general rule, when there are competing claims, reality often falls somewhere in between the extremes advocated by the Pollyannas and the Chicken Littles. Of course, it is still useful to pay attention to the source of funding. Papers published in peer-reviewed journals list funding sources and authors' potential conflicts of interests. It should raise a red flag if there have been many studies and the only positive results come from an industry-funded study, or if there have been hundreds of studies with variable results, but a stakeholder keeps pointing to just a handful of studies with positive results (unless those are the only studies that fit certain quality criteria, such as size or adequate controls). Because scientists at government agencies are sometimes pressured to dilute their conclusions about highly politicized issues such as global climate change, it is also important to pay attention to political forces that may distort scientific results.

Up to this point in the chapter, the discussion has focused on two questions. What forces decide what science gets done? How do external influences shape the process of science? On the other side of the reciprocal relationship between science and policy are the questions regarding what to do about the science once the results or new technologies are in hand. What is the best course of action for health, environmental, economic, or ethical reasons? What forces shape the decisions? These questions form the basis of the remainder of the chapter.

From scientific results to policy decisions—more morals and money

Global warming, genetically engineered crops, nanotechnology, drug safety, biofuels, infectious diseases, loss of biodiversity, and use of embryonic stem cells are just a few of the many scientific issues in the limelight around the world today. The regulatory agencies of many nations as well as international organizations are engaged in making decisions about these issues, while scientists continue to research outstanding questions about them. As a result, new policies often must be developed on the basis of incomplete or uncertain scientific information. When the science is unclear, policymakers are faced with at least two layers of judgment and interpretation. First, they must sort through the available scientific studies, interpret conflicting findings, and determine how much weight to assign to each study. In doing so, they come up with what they consider to be a realistic list of risks and benefits of making one policy decision or another. Second, once they decide what tradeoffs exist, they must make value judgments about what risks are acceptable tradeoffs for what benefits.

Public discussions of values in science typically focus on whether science is being conducted in an ethical manner. Are experimental subjects being treated with dignity? Is the reporting of the research free of deliberate attempts to mislead? Does the nature of the research clash with people's religious values? Less public discussion is devoted to the roles played by ethical considerations in decisions made on the basis of the science. To be sure, there are many disputes about policy decisions, but these disputes do not usually clarify the underlying value judgments driving the decisions. Yet, by definition, the term "tradeoff" means that something is lost when something is gained. Determining what risks and benefits exist can be done relatively objectively, as discussed in the previous chapters, but trading off risks and benefits to make a decision is a subjective process. Faced with the same tradeoffs in life, we do not all make the same decisions. Some people face long commutes to and from work for the opportunity to have a nice house in the suburbs. Others, with a similar family and financial situation, choose instead to rent an apartment or townhouse within easy commuting distance of their jobs. Some people are willing to face the expense and health risks of cosmetic surgery, while other similarly attractive people would not consider it. Some couples who are unable to conceive a child opt for international adoptions, while other couples of similar means and circumstances do not.

One for all

Given the dramatic differences in the life decisions people make in the face of the same tradeoffs, what principles are used to ensure that policy decisions, some of which have the potential to affect every citizen around the world, are as fair as possible? What is even meant by fair? In his famous paper, "The Tragedy of the Commons," Garrett Hardin pointed out that most individuals will not voluntarily give up something that they feel is in their best interests (for example, having another child) when the damage it does to the "commons"—shared resources—is small, perhaps even invisible to them. The "Tragedy of the Commons," which was published in *Science* in 1968, argued that restricting individual freedom was acceptable and necessary when it was for the greater good. Hardin was making the case for population control, but his logic can be used to argue for many of the rules that restrict the freedoms of individuals and private enterprises, including laws against littering, bans on smoking in public places, tougher emission standards for vehicles, water use restrictions during droughts, and leash laws for pets. In each case, these policies sacrifice the good of the minority for the good of the majority, and most people would agree that the sacrifices are worth the benefits.

However, other situations exist in which taking action to do the greatest good for the greatest number of people would lead to strong moral objections from many. Spending a million dollars or more to save one premature baby in the developed world is not doing the greatest good for the greatest number of individuals, when that same amount of money could provide the basic sanitation and health care that would save thousands of children in developing nations. Still, few people would feel comfortable ending the care that could save the life of the premature baby. Similarly, not many people would feel comfortable with making it a policy to execute criminals so that their organs could be used to save the lives of people waiting for organ transplants. The point of these examples is not to delve into complex philosophies of justice, but rather to show that any approach to balancing tradeoffs, no matter how reasonable it is in some situations, simply cannot be applied to all situations. No one-size-fits-all approach exists. In addition, when an issue involves more than one theme of tradeoff, even defining "good" becomes an issue. Good for human health? Good for the environment? Good for the economy or our own pocket books?

A cautionary tale of false positives and false negatives

Parents love to tell their kids "better safe than sorry" to coerce them to take a sweater, to not ride their bike wearing flip-flops, or to look both ways before crossing the road. Those words sometimes echo in our heads because the cautious thing to do is obvious, even when we opt not to do it. But in designing medical and environmental tests, the most cautious approach is not obvious. No test is perfect. There is always a chance of false positives and false negatives.

- A false positive is when the test tells you that you have the disease, when you are healthy, or indicates that a chemical is present in the environment, when it is not.

- A false negative is a test that tells you that you are healthy when you have the disease, or indicates that a chemical is not present in the environment, when it is present.

Those who design and analyze such tests try to be as accurate as possible, but for borderline results, they have to err on the side of caution. That's tricky though because whether a false positive or a false negative is erring on the side of caution depends on what you are testing for. Is it worse to accuse a business of discharging a chemical illegally when it is not, or to fail to catch a polluter? Is it worse for a DNA test to permit a criminal to go free or to condemn an innocent man? Is it worse to be told you are pregnant when you are not, or the other way around?

Always ask for a second opinion! Better safe than sorry.

The precautionary principle

The precautionary principle is an approach to decision-making that has been used internationally in many declarations and treaties. A controversial application of the precautionary principle was the European Union's use of it to prohibit the cultivation and importation of genetically engineered food. The basic premise of the precautionary principle is that any technology or procedure with the potential to harm the environment or

human health should not be introduced until it is proven to be completely safe. The decision to block the introduction of an innovation does
not have to be based on scientific proof that it causes harm. Instead, in
the face of scientific uncertainty, the precautionary principle places the
onus on the party that opposes the ban to prove that the innovation will
not cause harm.

Like basing a decision on doing the greatest good for the greatest
number of people, taking a "better safe than sorry" approach is ethically
appealing. In fact, the precautionary principle subsumes the one for all
approach because it puts the health of the commons—the environment—and the health of the populace above the profits of corporations.
The problem with the precautionary principle is that no innovation can
be proven to be completely safe. Not only would it take a very long time
for innovations to be introduced if long-term environmental and human
health studies were required prior to their introduction—no innovation
is completely safe. As discussed in Chapter 3, "Decisions, Decisions,"
genetically modified crops have potential risks associated with them, but
so do conventionally grown crops and organic crops. In other words, the
precautionary principle paints a black-and-white picture, ignoring the
shades of grey and splashes of color that are the norm for any complex
decision. It holds innovations to a higher standard than the status quo,
because it aims to classify the innovation as safe/not safe without placing
it in the context of its alternatives. To make a decision based on the precautionary principle is to ignore the elements of good decision-making
discussed in Chapter 3. Sound decisions are based on the careful analysis
of all the risks/costs and benefits that have been elucidated within the
appropriate context.

Costs benefits analysis

The costs benefits analysis approach to decision-making can incorporate
the strengths of one for all and the precautionary principle, while over-
coming the weaknesses in these approaches. In keeping with one for all,
the possibility of doing the most good for the greatest number of people
can be factored in as a potential benefit of a course of action. In keeping
with the precautionary principle, the possibility of causing irreparable
harm to the environment can be factored in as a potential risk of a course
of action. However, the costs benefits analysis does not stop there. The

options must be laid out and considered according to their health and well-being, environmental and economic costs and benefits. The costs benefits analysis is therefore the most complete approach to decision-making.

When assessing a policy, it is important to determine whether it is based on a costs benefits analysis or the precautionary principle. Table 8.4 illustrates how costs benefits analyses lead to more nuanced decisions than the precautionary principle. For instance, a costs benefits analysis sometimes turns one decision into a set of decisions to optimize the outcome in each situation.

TABLE 8.4   Comparison of a costs benefits analysis and the precautionary principle

Issue	Precautionary principle	Costs benefits analysis
Genetically engineered food	Prohibit commercial cultivation and importation until completion of long-term human health and environmental trials.	Evaluate on a crop-by-crop basis, compared to alternatives. Test, monitor, or prohibit crops with particular concerns (such as potential allergic reactions when genes have been swapped between very different species).
Global climate change	Implement all technically feasible methods to reduce greenhouse gas emissions regardless of economic implications.	Provide economic stimuli for the development of alternative energy sources and to encourage conservation. Force large emitters of greenhouse gases to reduce emissions, but only to the extent possible without having jobs outsourced to countries with lower environmental standards.
Bisphenol A	Ban it until it is proven to cause no harm to health.	For each BPA application, compare available alternatives and only replace BPA if a safer, technically feasible alternative exists.

TABLE 8.4   continued

Issue	Precautionary principle	Costs benefits analysis
Antidepressants	Mandate warning labels, but also educate the public. Closely monitor children and adolescents prescribed antidepressants.	Warn physicians and educate the public. Closely monitor children and adolescents prescribed antidepressants.

Of course, you will not necessarily agree with a decision even if it is based on a costs benefits analysis. People have different views about how much risk/cost is acceptable in exchange for what benefits. For example, some people are willing to put their nation's economic competitiveness at risk to protect the environment, but others are not. Others reason differently about risks over which they have control—such as not wearing a seatbelt—than risks over which they feel they do not have control—such as pesticides in drinking water.

Changing societal concerns can also influence how risks and benefits are weighed. The risk of catastrophe and the difficulties of disposing of radioactive waste made nuclear energy unpopular, but lately nuclear energy has been promoted as a green alternative to the burning of fossil fuels. The concerns about nuclear energy have not been alleviated, but factoring global warming into the equation changed how some people weigh the tradeoffs. Therefore, a costs benefits analysis applied to the same body of knowledge, but using different values leads to different conclusions about the best course of action (see Figure 8.1). In deciding on the merits of a proposed policy, we need to decide whether our own values, applied to the same body of knowledge, would result in the same conclusion. Doing this effectively means we also need to recognize weaknesses in our own reasoning processes that may trip us up. Reasoning foibles, including the tactics stakeholders use to get past our logical defenses, are the focus of the next chapter.

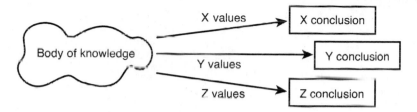

FIGURE 8.1 Subjectivity in decision-making

Key features of the reciprocal relationship between science and society

- All citizens can have a voice in what research gets funded.

- When interpreting research findings, it is important to be aware of the source of the research funding, which can bias the results and the conclusions.

- Results of different studies on a complex issue may vary widely, especially if the effects being observed are relatively subtle. When results are all over the map, the truth is often closer to the middle than to one extreme or the other.

- There are various models of decision-making. The precaution-ary principle is used frequently, but it has the disadvantage of being rather black and white. Proving zero risk is impossible, and the analysis is incomplete if the risks and benefits of the alternatives are not taken into consideration.

- Even when the science is in hand, not everyone is going to come to the same conclusion about what should be done. It depends on individual values about how much risk and what kind of risk is acceptable in exchange for what benefits.

9

All the tricks in the book: get past the ploys designed to simply bypass logic

One day in my high school biology class, our teacher passed between the rows of students to hand each of us a small strip of paper. "When I count to three, touch the paper to your tongue," he instructed us. Immediately following the count of three, many of the students started moaning, "Ew. Yuck. That's disgusting." In contrast, I could not taste anything, even when I started gnawing on my strip. I assumed that some students had been given gross tasting paper while the rest of us had received plain paper, but I was wrong. The teacher explained that we had each received a strip of paper impregnated with a chemical called phenylthiocarbamide (PTC). For those who can detect it, PTC tastes horribly bitter. However, due to a small genetic difference, some of us lack a taste receptor—a protein in our taste buds that detects PTC. That tiny, invisible difference separated us into PTC "tasters" and "nontasters" and ensured that our subjective experiences of that high school biology class were very different. As the tasters' faces screwed up with disgust, the nontasters laughed in surprise and amusement at the reactions of their peers. The point of the PTC demonstration was to introduce important concepts in genetics, but that was not what kept us all talking about it after class. It was also a profound demonstration that reality could deceive us— that we experience the world in fundamentally different ways without realizing it. Nevertheless, objective reality is not just the average of a mosaic of individual realities. PTC exists. If we want to detect it, but cannot taste it, there are various methods to test for it in a chemistry laboratory. In other words, when we know about our limitations, we can find ways to overcome them.

The inability to taste PTC is not much of a disadvantage. On the contrary, those of us who cannot taste certain bitter chemicals are less likely to turn up our noses at Brussels sprouts, spinach, and broccoli, which contain them. However, plenty of other characteristics predispose us to perceive the world in certain ways and interfere with our ability to make balanced decisions. This chapter focuses on the ways logic can break down during the decision-making process. The first section examines common flaws in logic. In doing so, it revisits key concepts introduced in previous chapters. The remainder of the chapter explores the many techniques that stakeholders use to bypass logic entirely. Because decision-making is so important to individuals and society, there is considerable scientific research on the (foibles) of human reasoning. Knowing about some of the major findings of this research can help you get to know your own biases and vulnerabilities in the face of efforts to influence you, and will make you more resistant to persuasive ploys.

(margin note: lack, flaws, deficiency)

Quirks of logic

Our brains have evolved to process information in ways that simplify our lives. For example, they automatically tune out the irrelevant details of our environment. It would be difficult to focus on a conversation if we could not tune out background noise, or to get from point A to point B if we paid equal attention to everything in our visual fields, rather than focusing on what is relevant to our safety. Of course, if we want to focus on the background sounds, or the beauty of our surroundings, we can consciously choose to do so. The tendency of our brains to try to make things simple also results in quirks of logic. Conscious effort can help us overcome the quirkiness once we know how to change our focus.

Failure to think outside the box

A simple psychology experiment reveals that people have trouble reasoning outside the box—literally. In the experiment, people are given a small box, a candle, thumbtacks, and a few other items and are asked to find a way to mount the candle on a wall. The items are presented in one of two ways. People are either handed the box with the other items inside, or they are just given all the items including the empty box. In both cases, the experimental subjects have the same problem to solve and the same array of items available to solve it. Yet how the items are presented strongly affects performance. When people receive the empty box along with the other items, they quickly figure out that they can make a shelf from the box, thumbtack it to the wall and place the candle on it. It takes them much longer to find this solution if when they received the box, it was serving as a container for the other items. In other words, when something is presented in one context, it is difficult for people to see it in another context.

The failure to think outside the box is not constrained to puzzles dreamed up in a psychology laboratory. Stepping back and seeing the big picture context, as discussed in detail in Chapter 3, "Decisions, Decisions," and Chapter 4, "Compare and Contrast," is a key component of evaluating any new technology, policy, or procedure. However, the media often fails to present the whole picture, and stakeholders can deliberately select an inappropriate context for comparison to present their option in the most favorable light. If we are provided with one context, we may not automatically stretch our minds to generate other possible contexts, but by acknowledging this weakness in our reasoning processes and becoming familiar with the contexts presented in Chapters 3 and 4, thinking outside the box can become second nature.

Predisposition to link cause and effect

The ability to determine that something caused something else is so critical to survival that nearly all creatures great and small are predisposed to make such connections. Fruit flies easily learn to avoid an odor that has been previously paired with a shock. Bees learn to fly to tiles of a specific color when they have previously received a reward of sugar water on tiles of that color. Tobacco hornworm caterpillars that learned to avoid an odor paired with a shock also avoided that odor as adults, even though metamorphosis into an adult moth involves a dramatic rearrangement of the nervous system. Rats avoid food of a certain flavor if food with that flavor made them sick just once, and even if the flavor (added by tricky researchers) was not the cause of their illness. Pigeons learn to do the jig when bits of food are dropped into their cages at regular intervals, because they superstitiously interpret their movements as being the cause of the food's sudden appearance.

Humans have the same tendency to assume that things occurring in the same time frame are linked by cause rather than coincidence. Stakeholders exploit our tendency to leap to conclusions about the link between cause and effect by presenting anecdotes and poorly designed studies to prove their claims about the merits of a product or the drawbacks of a decision. Getting past the knee-jerk reaction to link cause and effect is not easy, but together with the awareness that we all have this tendency, the concepts discussed in Chapter 5, "What Happens If...?," including types of confounding factors, the merits of combining multiple forms of data, and the importance of mechanisms, can go a long way in helping you resist efforts to pull the wool over your eyes.

Overgeneralization

We are all lumpers. We like to put things in categories and draw conclusions about the category rather than drawing separate conclusions for each of its components. In many ways, putting things in categories makes it easier for us to function, but we frequently overgeneralize. People even confuse entire issues by lumping them together with unrelated issues. For example, studies reveal that people, even college science majors, make many inappropriate connections between different environmental issues. To be sure, real relationships exist between global warming, pollution, loss of biodiversity, and other environmental problems. However, one study revealed that lumping was often taken to an extreme. For example, the majority of people in the study thought global warming would lead to an increase in the prevalence of skin cancer. They had applied their knowledge about the consequences of damage to the ozone layer to the problems associated with the increase in the levels of greenhouse gases, but these are distinct issues.

Not only do flawed conclusions result from lumping together different issues, but as discussed in Chapter 6, "Specific or General," overgeneralization within a single issue can also be misleading. Within each issue, variation exists across different individuals, locations, conditions, and periods of time. As a result, sophisticated decisions are not based on the highly polarized options presented to us by many stakeholders (for example, ban or not ban genetically engineered food), but rather on the options that take into consideration the differences within categories (for example, select the method of farming that is most suitable for each crop, and recognize that the best method could vary depending on the type of crop).

Strange ways our minds make sense of statistics

Studies have shown that people often reason about statistics in quirky ways. The Gambler's Fallacy is a good example. After several coin tosses that result in heads, people assume they are "due" for tails, or after several consecutive wheel spins that land on red, gamblers assume they are due for black. Doing so confuses the odds against a sequence with the odds against an event in that sequence. Each toss or spin is independent of the previous one. In other words, previous outcomes do not somehow influence future outcomes. A run of heads or reds is not a sign of something supernatural at work. The sequence THHHHIIH is just as likely as the sequence THTHHTH. The former is simply more likely to jump out at us because we are predisposed to honing in on patterns. Our propensity for pattern recognition also trips us up outside of Vegas and Monte Carlo. As discussed in Chapter 7, "Fun Figures," it gives rise to funky headlines about trends. Crime, accidents, and "outbreaks" of noncontagious diseases are all featured in headlines about trends. The headlines heighten people's awareness about incidents that they would usually ignore, and this further fuels the trend frenzy. Be suspicious of supposed trends. Unless they are strong and there is a good explanation for them, they are probably normally occurring fluctuations in data.

Another quirk of statistical reasoning is that when numbers are presented in terms of the *costs* of making one choice or another, we sometimes reason differently than when the mathematically identical statistics are presented in terms of the *benefits* of making one choice or another. In one study, researchers presented a problem in which the United States was getting prepared for the outbreak of an unusual Asian disease expected to kill 600 people. The researchers gave two options for battling the disease: option A, which would save 200 lives, and option B, with which there is a 1-in-3 chance that all 600 would be saved and a 2-in-3 chance that no one would be saved. Most people chose option A. However, the researchers found that if they phrased the options in terms of dying (costs) instead of living (benefits), people responded differently. In this case, the options were: option A, which would guarantee that 400 people die, and option B, with which there is a 1-in-3 chance that no one would die and a 2-in-3 chance that all 600 would die. This time, more people selected option B. The options did not change, but people's interpretations changed according to how the options were presented. As described in Chapter 4, reframing gains as losses and losses as gains can help you overcome this quirk of reasoning about statistics.

Getting dragged down by anchors

Arbitrary and irrelevant bits of information have a way of getting factored into our decisions, especially if the pieces of information are readily available. In the study that introduced this phenomenon—the so-called anchoring effect—people spun a "wheel of fortune" and then were asked to estimate what percentage of countries in the United Nations were African. Unbeknownst to them, the wheel was rigged to stop at 10 or 65. On average, people who saw the wheel stop at 10 guessed that 25 percent of the countries were African. The average estimate was 45 percent for people who saw the wheel stop at 65. In other words, people took irrelevant cues from the wheel. Similarly, people asked to read a list of words and then evaluate a young man in an ambiguous news story took cues from the irrelevant list of words. If the list contained several terms of praise, the man got a more favorable evaluation than if the list contained several negative terms. In another study in which people were asked to read lists composed of half male and half female names, they judged that most of the names were female if some of the female names were famous. If some of the male names were famous, then they judged that most of the names were male. These examples are all straight out of a psychology laboratory, but advertisers frequently use these kinds of associations to convince us that their product is a good deal—for example, by jacking up the price and then marking it down. Another way stakeholders exploit our tendency to make associations is by preceding a discussion of a product, policy, or candidate with irrelevant positive or negative images. It is difficult to stop making these associations because we make them unconsciously. However, we can recognize when stakeholders are deliberately presenting irrelevant information to sway our opinions and make a conscious effort to determine what our decision would be in the absence of that information.

Confirmation bias

Confirmation bias is responsible for keeping superstitions alive and nurturing beliefs in astrology. Confirmation bias is ubiquitous. We succumb to it when we pay attention to evidence that supports our beliefs while ignoring evidence to the contrary. Carefully choosing evidence with the intention of winning an argument is not confirmation bias. Confirmation bias acts at a subconscious level. So all the times a black cat crossed a superstitious person's path and nothing happened get forgotten, but the one time the crossing was followed by an unfortunate incident stands out in memory. All the ridiculous horoscopes get forgotten, but the one accurate horoscope grabs our attention. Confirmation bias makes us vulnerable to stakeholders who manipulate us by telling us what we want to hear.

The media often tells us what we want to hear to keep us engaged, or because reporters themselves have succumbed to confirmation bias in interpreting the studies that form the basis of their stories. The stories trumpeting that marriage makes people healthier and happier—as debunked by Bella DePaulo in her book *Singled Out: How Singles Are Stereotyped, Stigmatized, and Ignored, and Still Live Happily Ever After*—exemplify confirmation bias. College students estimate that they would be five points happier on a ten-point scale if they got married and stayed married than if they remained single. In contrast, studies of married and single people show that the difference is only about one-half point on a ten-point scale. Not only is the happiness difference very small, up to five years before their marriage, people who will later get married and stay married are already a fraction of a point happier than people who will get married and get divorced, or people who stay single. In other words, marriage does not seem to be the cause of the small happiness difference, but folk wisdom says it is, and the media uncritically present the data that confirm folk wisdom. Confirmation bias can be overcome by actively seeking counterexamples and evidence that conflicts with your viewpoint.

Hearts and guts

If stakeholders who do not have well-reasoned, evidence-based arguments want to convince you of something, clearly they need to make the appeal to you using something other than sound logic. They also need to prevent you from applying your best reasoning skills in response to their appeals. They have plenty of tricks at their disposal. They can make use of unsound logic, specifically playing into the weaknesses in our reasoning processes described previously, such as our propensity to leap to conclusions about cause and effect, our tendency to overgeneralize, or the way we pay extra attention to ideas that confirm our viewpoints. Alternatively, they can abandon any attempt to appeal to our minds and instead appeal to our emotions and gut reactions. They may play on our need to feel hip and cool, make us feel pity or outrage, embarrass us into submission, pretend they are letting us in on some secret wisdom, fill us with warm fuzzy feelings, tell us we have nothing to lose, or stereotype their opponents to make them seem undeserving of attention. These common attempts to bypass logic are the focus of the remainder of this chapter.

Beware of pseudo experts

Movie stars, sports heroes, and other celebrities make enormous amounts of money by endorsing products. They do song and dance routines, provide serious-sounding testimonials, or merely appear in an ad with a product. These ads work. Companies would not give celebrities multimillion-dollar endorsements if they were not paying off in increased sales revenue. Yet why should people be influenced by these ads? Sometimes the celebrities endorse a product about which they can legitimately claim to have expertise, such as a basketball star endorsing basketball shoes, but more often than not, the celebrity does not have any relevant expertise at all. Of course, paying a premium for a product endorsed by a celebrity, and then going out in public wearing or using the product, appeals to the desire to feel trendy and part of the in crowd. However, celebrities promote plenty of products that are not hip at all, such as medications, cleaning products, and kitty litter. Why are these marketing campaigns successful? People believe celebrities just because they are famous. Plus, the setting, lighting, music, and action are all selected to make the celebrity seem even larger than life. Marketers also use tricks to make unknown actors appear to be authorities. For example, they dress them in lab coats, or place them in a rugged outdoorsy setting or next to some impressive-looking, high-tech equipment. No mention is made of their credentials. They are simply placed in a scene that makes them appear to be experts. Ads turn the celebrity or the unknown actor into a pseudo expert.

Most people who are swayed to buy a product as a result of the endorsement of a celebrity or unknown actor would agree that the celebrity is not really an expert on it, but the same cannot be said for another type of pseudo expert—the victim as expert. People with various diseases, or parents of children with those diseases, are often featured on talk shows and quoted in the media. To be sure, they are experts on how to live with that disease and how it feels to suffer from that disease. However, they are not experts on the cause of that disease. They may be entirely sincere and completely convinced that exposure to some chemical caused their leukemia or their child's autism, but it is impossible for them to do anything but guess at the cause. After all, real experts have not pinpointed the cause of these and other complex diseases. Experts may know how much a person's risk of getting cancer may be increased as a result of exposure to a chemical, but they cannot examine a cell and conclude that the chemical caused it to become cancerous.

A victim who claims, "My disease was caused by X," is essentially drawing conclusions on the basis of a retrospective epidemiological study (Chapter 5) with only one member. Victims may tug at our heartstrings, but that is not a reason to avoid thinking critically about the claims they present as science. Bob, a hard-working salesman, may have used a cell phone frequently to stay in touch with customers and suppliers. Bob may have indeed died a gruesome death from brain cancer. His parents may be completely convinced that the cell phone caused his brain cancer. They may be down to earth and believable, but that does not make them right. After all, people died of brain cancer long before cell phones were ever invented. More than an anecdote is needed to make the link. No matter how heart wrenching or horrifyingly graphic victims' stories may be, an anecdote or series of anecdotes is never proof about a cause.

Another type of pseudo expert is the "masses." Stakeholders try to persuade us to buy products or ideas on the basis of the fact that large numbers of people have already been persuaded. "Ten thousand people have already preordered this miraculous antiaging remedy. What are you waiting for?" The power of numbers is comforting. (Ironically, there are always greater numbers of people who have not purchased the product or subscribed to the idea, but this fact gets conveniently ignored by the stakeholders.) It is tempting to hop on the bandwagon, especially when the other folks on the bandwagon are portrayed as everyday people like you and me—albeit the slightly hipper, cooler versions of ourselves that we strive to be. Needless to say, the masses are not always right. Stakeholders can trick the masses, and then use their supposed support to convince more people. For example, as discussed in Chapter 7, stakeholders can manipulate who answers surveys as well as how they answer. These rather artificial results can then be used to appeal to others to join the crowd.

Anyone who claims to have expertise about an issue but does not have the relevant credentials is a pseudo expert. Relevant credentials are not necessarily degrees; they may be extensive work or life experiences. Also, degrees are not always relevant credentials. Knowledge is specialized. Someone with a doctorate in genetics may have no more knowledge about astronomy than someone with a high school education. Those who have earned a doctorate in genetics will have a basic knowledge of other subfields in biology, but it may not be enough knowledge to make them a legitimate authority on topics in the subfields that are new, particularly controversial, or very technical. Be careful not to lose your willingness to be critical just because you hear someone introduced as Dr. so and so. Listen for mention of credentials that are relevant to the topic they are discussing. Legitimate experts are usually cautious about claiming authority outside their area of expertise.

Look out for buzzwords and slogans

How often do you hear advertisers use the words "all natural" or "chemical free?" The prevalence of such loaded terms is a testament to their power to sell products. Natural seems inherently virtuous. "All natural ingredients" or "ninety-nine percent natural" claims the label on a snack or a bottle of hand lotion. Clearly, this is meant to imply that the product is good for you. However, unlike the label "organic," which can be used only if the ingredients were grown in accordance with a set of rules specified (in the United States) by the Department of Agriculture, there are few rules specifying how the word "natural" can be used. Therefore, the label "natural" says little about how the product was grown and/or prepared. Even if the label could be trusted to mean "from nature," it still would not necessarily mean the product is more healthful. Plenty of things that come from animals, plants, or the earth are unhealthy, such as lard, tobacco, and arsenic.

"Chemical-free" is an even more misleading term. Reporters and the public often fall into the trap of believing that chemicals are inherently bad. For example, one newspaper article praised a new "chemical-free" sunscreen that contained titanium dioxide, "a mineral that reflects the sun's harmful UVA and UVB rays." The claim is ridiculous. Minerals are chemicals. In fact, nothing is free of chemicals because everything, including food, water, and our bodies, is made from some combination of chemical elements found in the periodic table of the elements. It is possible for a product to be free of synthetic chemicals, which means that none of the chemicals in the product was synthesized in a laboratory. However, it is inaccurate to think of nonsynthetic and synthetic chemicals as a good/bad dichotomy. Some nonsynthetic chemicals, such as the oil in poison oak and poison ivy that causes rashes, are dangerous to your health, and some synthetic chemicals, including novel antibiotics, can be life saving. Also, the processes used to make synthetic chemicals are not necessarily more damaging to the environment than the processes used to make nonsynthetic chemicals. For example, if the nonsynthetic chemicals need to be extracted from wild plants, overcollection can impact these species. The distinction between synthetic and nonsynthetic can even get a bit tenuous because the extraction of the nonsynthetic chemical may involve considerable processing after the raw material is harvested or mined.

Modern synthetic methods can create compounds including vitamins and drugs that are identical to the ones found in nature with respect to their chemistry and effects on the body. It may be cheaper to synthesize a compound than to extract it from a plant, because it may take a ton of plant material to extract a few pounds of the compound of interest. It is also sometimes possible to synthesize a modified version of a compound that is more effective than the one Mother Nature provided or has fewer side effects. For example, a synthetic compound has been designed that is a modified version of artemisinin—an antimalarial drug extracted from the bark of the sweet wormwood tree, which has been used in Chinese medicine for 1,500 years. Not only is the new compound a potent treatment for malaria, but because the modifications reduce the rate at which it degrades in the bloodstream, it does not have to be administered to patients as often as artemisinin. These examples are not meant to suggest that synthetic is always better than nonsynthetic. The whole point is that regardless of what stakeholders might like you to believe, the clear good/bad dichotomy is misleading.

In addition to terms such as "natural" and "chemical free" that appeal almost subconsciously to our notions of goodness, advertisers use other labels and slogans to take advantage of the latest fads. For example, low-fat labels were the norm in the 1980s and 1990s when most people believed a healthy diet meant minimizing fat intake. Later, with the rise in popularity of the carbohydrate conscious diets, such as the South Beach diet and the Atkins diet, advertisers leapt on the new bandwagon and began emphasizing the low carbohydrate content of their snacks. Unfortunately, these labels do not say anything about a product's effects on health. The low-fat products may be full of sugar, and the low-carbo-hydrate products may be high in saturated fat. Of course, regulatory agencies, including the U.S. Food and Drug Administration, mandate that ingredients and detailed nutritional information be listed on all food products, so people can read the list of ingredients, check the grams of saturated fat and sugar, and see how many vitamins and minerals the product provides. The problem is that people often interpret the low-fat or low-carb labels to mean that the product is good for them. Claims on packaging are designed to sell a product, and appealing to our inherent sense of good and health is a way to trick us into buying without reflecting.

Labels on packaging are so powerful that Monsanto embarked on a lengthy legal battle in an attempt to prevent dairy producers from using labels to indicate that their products came from cows not given bovine growth hormone (BGH). Since Monsanto spent $300 million perfecting the technique of injecting cows with BGH to make them produce more milk, the company had significant stake in preventing unfavorable con-sumer opinion about BGH. Monsanto's argument was that the labels, which merely stated that BGH was not used in the production of certain milk, insinuated that BGH was unsafe. Monsanto launched the lawsuit because the company knew that labels influence consumers' decisions, whether or not the labels provide sufficient detail for a consumer to make an informed decision. A consumer's gut reaction is that a company would not put information on a label if it is meaningless, so BGH-free must mean it is healthier. The compromise that came as a result of

Monsanto's legal battle can be found in the fine print on milk cartons in your grocery store. Milk can be labeled to indicate that it comes from cows that were not injected with BGH, but milk so-labeled must also display a statement that milk from cows injected with BGH does not differ from milk from cows not injected with BGH.

Slogans and buzzwords are not constrained to advertisements and labels, but are a favorite tool of stakeholders to push forward a variety of agendas. The slogans used by today's western political leaders may not be as extreme as those used by the Party in George Orwell's *1984*, but slogans and buzzwords abound. For example, calling an initiative "Clear Skies" or "Healthy Forests" is a great way to ensure that voters' gut reactions will be favorable, regardless of the true implications of the initiatives. Similarly, antibiotech protesters have cleverly dubbed genetically modified foods "Frankenfoods" to evoke the fear of science out of control.

It is easy to change a negative into a positive or vice versa by playing with language. Table 9.1 lists the implied meaning of several commonly used buzzwords. Other examples abound. A leader is held in high esteem by supporters for having strong convictions, but criticized by opponents for being overly opinionated. A company advertises its product as light and economical, while the competition disparages the product for being flimsy and cheap. Language can also be used ambiguously to permit people to hear what they want to hear. "You can be sure your concerns will be given the attention they deserve," may mean that your concerns will initiate a careful investigation or that they will be utterly ignored. Of course, we generally assume such a statement means the former. Grammatical errors and misuse of punctuation can also completely alter the meaning of a statement; although these tend to be humorous accidents rather than attempts at manipulation. *Eats, Shoots and Leaves* is a book about punctuation that exploits a misuse of punctuation in its title. It came from a poorly punctuated statement about the dietary habits of giant pandas. The statement conjures up the image of a gun-toting, dine and dash sort of creature, rather than a sedate vegetarian.

TABLE 9.1   Buzzwords and their implied meaning

Buzzword	Meaning
Natural	Healthier
Chemical free	Safer/healthier
Synthetic	Unnatural
Low fat	Healthier
Low carb	Healthier
Frankenfoods	Dangerous
All new	Better
Long tradition	More trustworthy
The establishment	Conspirators
Change	Improvement/antiestablishment
Simple	Wholesome
Pure	Healthier/safer

This section introduced just a few of the many buzzwords and slogans we come across daily, but it becomes progressively easier to identify catchy phrases that are meant to sell a product or idea once you get in the habit of looking out for them. It is useful to ask yourself what the stakeholder using a buzzword or slogan intends to imply and what can prudently be concluded about the meaning of the buzzword or slogan in the context in which it is being used. It is also important to consider whether the policy or product hidden behind the catchy words lives up to the feel-good nature of a positive slogan or is really as terrible as a negative slogan implies. Applying this kind of logic makes it more difficult for stakeholders to appeal to people's emotions without providing reasonable arguments.

Remember the story of "The Emperor's New Clothes"

In the children's story, "The Emperor's New Clothes," some con men breeze into town and convince an emperor that they can make him the finest clothes that anyone has seen, or not seen, as the case may be. The clothes are supposedly so fine that they can only be seen by intelligent people. One glance separates the wheat from the chaff, so to speak. Now, why the emperor would want stupid people to see him naked, I never understood, but the point is, the whole thing was a sham. The con men were extraordinarily convincing, weaving with their empty looms and miming the handling of the exquisite fabric, and the emperor fell for their ploy hook, line, and sinker. When the "clothes" were brought before him, he was too ashamed to admit that he could not see them. So he played along. For the same reason, the members of his court played along too. It was not until the emperor organized a parade to show off his new duds that he realized the con men were laughing all the way to the bank while he was showing off his family jewels in public. "Why isn't the emperor wearing any clothes?" asked a little kid. Suddenly everyone realized that they were not too dumb to see the emperor's clothes; the clothes actually did not exist.

No one wants to seem stupid. When a stakeholder implies that the ideas being used in an argument are obvious and should be understood by everyone, not many people want to step forward and ask for an explanation, just as no one wanted to admit they could not see the emperor's clothes. The use of excessive jargon is a similar tactic with a similar result. It is important to point out that terminology is not the same as jargon. Using precise names and descriptions of things helps scientists communicate. There is no everyday name for the medulla or the hypothalamus. Use of these words—which describe parts of the brain— is not a deliberate attempt to blind people with science. In contrast, the use of technical terms when plain language would do just fine is often a deliberate attempt to beat potential critics into submission. The next time your boss wants you to stay late at work, respond that you would love to, but that you are concerned about the potential comportment of the large, omnivorous, domesticated quadruped for which you find yourself responsible. It sounds a lot better than saying you have to go home before your dog tears the house apart.

Claims of ancient wisdom unknown to science should be treated as suspect

Modern scientists recognize that many native people around the world have a sophisticated knowledge of natural resources that has been passed down from generation to generation. Scientists from universities and industry alike are interested in this knowledge because it can provide leads to compounds with the potential to become effective treatments for cancer and other diseases, or that could be useful in important technological processes. For example, one San Diego-based company is studying the enzymes found in the guts of South American termites that help the termites digest wood and extract energy from it. The company hopes to use the knowledge to improve the efficiency of processes that make ethanol from scrap wood, crop waste, and other plant-derived material.

It is precisely because many scientists are interested in this kind of knowledge that claims about products with "powerful ingredients based on the ancient medical practices of culture X" that will cure all that ails you, or similar claims about ancient wisdom unknown to our culture, should be regarded with skepticism. Like buzzwords and slogans, claims that we can share in ancient wisdom that will improve our lives are attractive at a basic emotional level. People have a habit of being senti- mental about the past—"the good ole days"—while vilifying the present. Such attitudes predispose people to believe that knowledge has been lost on the route to modernity. Yet, it is curious that the only people who know about these amazing medical treatments, or other products sup- posedly based on ancient wisdom, are obscure individuals or companies that are making big bucks selling them through mail order catalogs or on the Internet. Despite what these people often claim, there is no chance that there is a great conspiracy among scientists to keep people from knowing about a wonderful product. The scientific community has noth- ing to gain from doing so. One pharmaceutical company might feel threatened by the discovery of a compound that could compete against its blockbuster drug, but it could not stifle research by scientists at other companies or universities, so the existence of the new compound would not remain secret for long.

If the San Diego company that is studying termite guts made a dis- covery that led to the development of a new process to make ethanol from wood, it would announce the exciting news to the public. It would keep the exact details of the process a secret and apply for a patent on it, but the company executives would want people to know about their dis- covery because good news makes shareholders happy and attracts invest- ment. To attract investment, the company would have to prove that its process works by putting it into practice. On the other hand, the snake oil salesman selling his mysterious cure-all is under no such scrutiny. Even if there are just a handful of satisfied customers (who responded because of the placebo effect), out of hundreds or thousands of dissatisfied customers, he can use the favorable testimonials about how this "wonderful treatment based on ancient wisdom" changed their lives to find new customers. Therefore, while ancient wisdom exists, it is unlikely that there is a secret unknown to everyone in the western world except the person trying to hawk a product purportedly based on that ancient wisdom.

Beware of vague, simple claims

You must make a distinction between something which has been made simple (stripped to its essence), and something which has been made simplistic (stripped of its essence).

—Alistair B. Fraser, Penn State University, Bad Meteorology Web site

Another tactic used by stakeholders to convince others of their position is to make broad, unspecific claims that sound like a good idea but are lacking in detail. This tactic is common in the political realm. Simple sound bites are often used to promote policies. For example, a lawyer at a farmer's market in Berkeley, California, asked for my signature to get his initiative onto the upcoming election ballot. The initiative would have made it illegal to sell coffee that was not organic, or fair trade, within the city of Berkeley.

Although the measure was ethically appealing, I wanted to know more about how the change to organic methods of growing coffee would affect farmers, and what chemicals would be used on the organic coffee farms. Specifically, what types of synthetic pesticides were currently being used, and were the nonsynthetic pesticides that would replace them safer? I asked these questions twice, a week apart, and on neither occasion was this activist able to answer. It is remarkable to me that someone would spend so much time and money on something about which he was not well informed. Even more surprising to me is that enough people provided signatures to get the measure on the ballot— apparently, given his surprise at my questions and his failure to do the research even after I posed the questions—without asking him to provide the finer details of the plan.

Claims about the merits of prescription drugs are also often vague. In recent years in the United States, there has been a dramatic increase in the number of direct to consumer advertisements for prescription medications. One San Diego radio announcer tracked the drug commercials during two hours of prime time television and found that 22 different medications were advertised during that time period. The commercials showed happy, healthy, active people, some of whom claimed that a drug had changed their lives, but the ads almost never said what ailment the drug treated. After watching the commercials, the radio announcer had no idea what nearly all of the drugs were meant to do. It seems odd that drug companies would spend millions of dollars on advertisements and not even tell people what ailments the drugs alleviated.

The explanation lies in a U.S. Food and Drug Administration rule that prohibits drug companies from advertising what condition their product is designed to treat, unless they also provide the complete list of side effects of their product. Rather than tell people about the risks of cramps, diarrhea, excessive belching, headaches, or any number of other possible side effects, many drug companies choose advertisements that promote name recognition associated with positive feelings, rather than education. They want patients to encourage their doctors to prescribe them the drug. By law, patients must be provided with a list of side effects when they fill a prescription for their drug, so all patients receive this information. However, once people ask their doctor to write a prescription, and go to the pharmacy to get it filled, they are probably less likely to carefully weigh the drug's risks and benefits than they would have been if they had heard about the drug's drawbacks as soon as they heard about its benefits.

Therefore, beware; if a claim is vague, there is probably a good reason you are not being provided with all the details you need to make an informed decision. Very likely, the stakeholders are withholding information about the possible drawbacks of the decision they so desperately want you to make. Instead, they rely on their ability to fill you with warm, fuzzy feelings about a product or policy, in the hope that those warm fuzzy feelings will encourage you to act without reflecting.

Claims that there are no disadvantages (or no advantages) should raise hackles

"You've got nothing to lose!" We often hear such claims from people encouraging us to buy things and sign up for special offers. They appeal to our deep-rooted desire to get a good deal. Yet, if others have something to gain, which they must if they are spending time and money on promotions, we probably have something to lose. A few win-win situations do exist. For example, by conserving energy, a business can help the environment and its bottom line, but, even then, an initial cash outlay is needed to implement the energy conservation measures. Most of us are indeed suspicious of hucksters telling us that we have nothing to lose. At the same time, our skepticism falls by the wayside when it comes to new medications or technological solutions to personal or societal problems. Disadvantages to what seemed like a great idea still come as a surprise. Indeed, risks and disadvantages can be difficult to predict.

When we went through our teenage growth spurts and were driven by insatiable hunger to raid the fridge and cupboards on a regular basis, many of our parents wondered aloud if we had worms. Worm infections are still a serious problem in developing countries. They used to be common in the developed world as well. Improvements in hygiene, especially sewage treatment programs, and the availability of clean drinking water have dramatically reduced the occurrence of worm infections in humans in the United States and other industrialized nations. It seems like a good thing to be carrying around fewer parasites, and anyone embarking on a program to reduce worm infections would not meet resistance (other than from the worms). However, the reduction in worm infections has come with an unanticipated health risk. In countries where intestinal worm infections are common, inflammatory bowel disease is rare. As worm infections have become more unusual in developed nations, inflammatory bowel disease has been on the rise. Researchers investigating the connection say that the worms may play a protective role by distracting the immune system. The distraction protects against the inflammation characteristic of inflammatory bowel disease by preventing the immune system from attacking the intestines themselves. As this example shows, even the most sensible actions can have unforeseen consequences. Therefore, claims that anything is free of risks or disadvantages should be taken with a grain of salt. Claims that insinuate there are no advantages to a course of action should also be treated with skepticism. There are always tradeoffs to be weighed.

Use caution when considering attacks by one stakeholder on another

Stakeholders often take advantage of people's affinity for simple arguments by attacking the competing position rather than presenting the evidence for their own position. This is a popular strategy because it is easier to find a weak link in someone else's argument than to explain the intricacies of one's own. Even a well-reasoned argument usually has some uncertainties that leave it open to attack. Opponents can be put on the defensive when attention is directed at the small uncertainties in their arguments, or through the more unscrupulous tactic of character attacks that move the attention away from the issue. Research indicates that negative information has more power to persuade people than positive information. Political campaigns spend millions of dollars on attack ads designed to discredit a political opponent's views and/or integrity. Since it would be complicated to attack multiple opponents and viewpoints simultaneously, attack ads are mostly used when there are only two candidates or only two viable candidates on the ballot. Under these circumstances, voters are often inundated with repetitious, superficial messages that provide few of the details needed to make an informed decision.

The intersection of religion and science is another area where attacks on the opposing position are often a substitute for clear articulation of the evidence for one's own position. For example, evolutionary biologists usually dislike debating proponents of intelligent design because, as described in Chapter 5, an understanding of evolution requires background information about genetics, ecology, molecular biology, morphology, and so on. While it is easy to launch an attack on evolution in a short sound bite, it is not easy to explain the evidence in favor of evolution in a series of sound bites. These debates make intelligent design seem inherently simpler and therefore more appealing, but this is misleading. For example, different proponents of intelligent design have different ideas about when the intelligent designer intervenes. Some believe the designer got things going and then stepped back, which means there is room for evolution to pick up where the designer left off. At the other end of the spectrum are those who propose that the intelligent designer created everything as is. These differences are not discussed when the debate consists of a series of attacks on evolution. Yet, the existence of these differences poses the same kinds of problems for intelligent design that disagreements between molecular biologists and paleontologists about species' ancestry pose for evolution.

The dihydrogen monoxide Web site introduced at the start of Chapter 2, "Who's Who?," also attacks the opposing position. The Web site reads, "In spite of overwhelming evidence, there is one group in California that opposes a ban on dihydrogen monoxide." The DHMO site presents the position statement of the group supposedly opposing the ban on DHMO. Then, instead of offering arguments against the position statement, DHMO.org raises issues about the funding source of the group opposing the ban. The funding source is supposed to be the "Scorched Earth Party," which is described as "radical and loosely-organized." Attacks by stakeholders on one another's integrity are so common and stereotypical that the DHMO Web site appears more realistic because it includes attacks like the ones used everyday by stakeholders in the real world.

Attacks on an opposing position are not always signs of a stakeholder being manipulative. Scientists criticize each other's work as well, and these challenges play a key role in the progress of science. However, certain features distinguish productive attacks and manipulative attacks. Productive attacks identify weaknesses but also acknowledge the strengths of the opposing position. They do not simply attack the motives or character of those in the opposing camp. They are explicit about what the weaknesses in the arguments are and how they could be addressed. They do not twist the opponents' position into an easy-to-knock-down straw man argument, for example, by deliberately overstating an opponent's position to make it appear extremist. They say what data would need to be collected to reduce their skepticism about certain conclusions. They are forthcoming about their own position and present their evidence for examination, rather than resorting to mantras and slogans to persuade others to adopt their point of view. They also reveal the sources of their evidence so that anyone interested can trace it back to its original source.

We encounter many examples where advertisements, political sound bites, and public relations campaigns have been carefully crafted to evoke positive gut reactions. By becoming aware of these tactics, we can train ourselves to get past the initial good/bad reflex, and seek the information necessary to ensure that a new technology really is an improvement over an old technology, that a piece of legislation is what it seems to be at face value, or that a product has real health benefits. This entails learning to recognize our flaws in logic (the failure to think outside the box, the predisposition to link cause and effect, overgeneralization, quirks in making sense of statistics, the influence of anchors, and confirmation bias), as well as the array of tricks used by stakeholders to bypass logic entirely (pseudo experts, buzzwords, slogans, jargon, vague claims, imaginary ancient wisdom, claims that you have nothing to lose, and manipulative attacks on opposing positions).

If a proposal sounds too good to be true, it probably is too good to be true. "Every decision has tradeoffs" is a great mantra. It is rare for something to benefit (or injure) environmental health, human health, and the economy at the same time. Most decisions result in winners and losers, or trade off short-term versus long-term benefits. Unfortunately, consumers of information often reward stakeholders for keeping it simple. For example, politicians who attempt to provide nuanced answers in debates are accused of waffling. Instead, we should demand that stakeholders present the full range of pros and cons. When they present unsubstantiated claims, it is time to ask tough questions to get the information needed to make balanced decisions. Sometimes the only way to get needed information is to seek it oneself. The final chapter in the book shows how the tools provided in the first nine chapters can be applied to new claims and controversies, and provides guidance on how and where to seek the information needed for balanced decision making.

10

Fitting the pieces together: know how to seek information to gain a balanced perspective

The most important product of knowledge is ignorance.

—David Gross, 2004 Nobel Laureate in Physics, at the annual University of California, San Diego Physics Department Memorial Lecture, April 21, 2005

Children are wide-eyed when they see a Russian Matryoshka doll for the first time. Inside the wooden doll is another, slightly smaller doll. Inside the smaller doll is yet another doll, and inside that one is another.... An impressive line of successively smaller dolls results when the dolls are de-nested. Even in an age of electronic gizmos and gadgets, this low-tech toy has the power to capture the imagination. There is something exciting about finding so many layers inside something that seems so simple. Like the Matryoshka dolls, science-related issues are composed of layers that can be de-nested. Peeling an onion or digging the fruit from a pomegranate are other metaphors for dissecting scientific issues. Perhaps the latter is the most appropriate metaphor because the tiny, ruby red fruits inside a pomegranate have a rather unpredictable arrangement like the jewels of knowledge in a scientific issue. Each jewel of knowledge is just a small part of a larger issue. It takes some peeling and digging to get to

the other jewels. The most important aspect of learning to reason critically about scientific issues is determining how to take stock of what you
know so that you can dig for what you do not know. The nine tools that
formed the basis of the first nine chapters make it easier to uncover gaps
in understanding because when you know what you are looking for, it is
easier to find. This chapter looks more closely at how clues in claims
make it possible to select and apply the appropriate tools. It also discusses where to find reliable information to facilitate decision-making
when you are confronted with new science-related issues.

Peeling back the layers

At the heart of any scientific issue is the process of science, including
how information came to be and the degree of consensus within the scientific community. Within, and one level out from the process of science,
are the conclusions drawn on the basis of the science. This level com-
prises whether the findings make it possible to distinguish definitively
between cause and coincidence, how broadly the conclusions can be
applied, and what is the most sensible interpretation of statistical information from the study. If information could be taken at face value
because no stakeholders were inadvertently or deliberately distorting it,
and there were no external influences on the process of science, there
would be just one more level—the decision-making level. It is the level
at which the pros and cons are elucidated and the alternatives are placed
in an appropriate context to evaluate tradeoffs. Of course, there are
external influences on the process of science, as well as stakeholders with
many ploys to distort scientific findings for their personal gain. Therefore, these external influences form yet another level, but they cannot be
neatly contained within a layer. They extend tendrils through each of the
other levels, as illustrated in Figure 10.1. Seeing past the tendrils and
determining the relevant information at each of the other levels is critical
to making sound decisions on science-based issues.

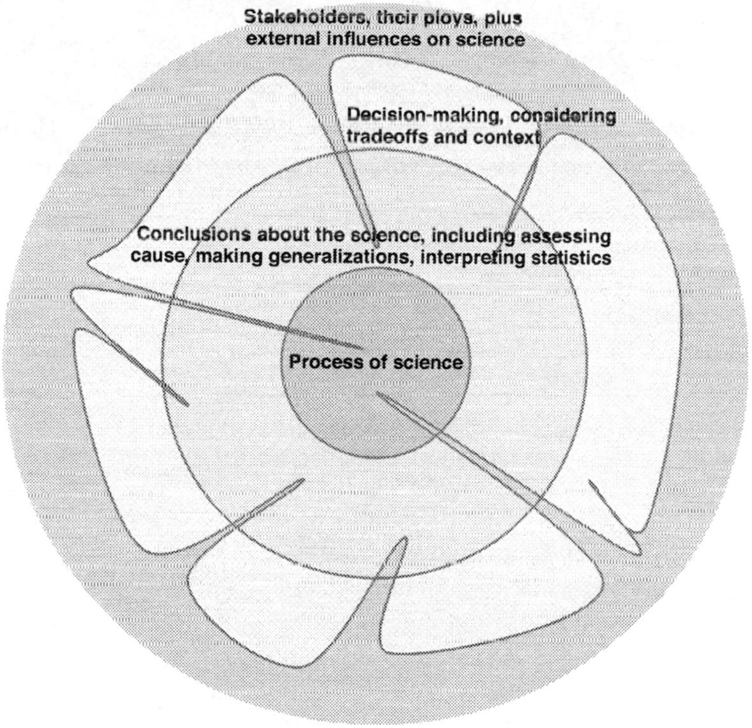

FIGURE 10.1 The many layers of scientific issues

Claims and caveats—case studies

Each chapter in this book introduced a different tool for reasoning about science-related issues. Of course, often multiple tools are relevant for making sense of a single issue, and part of the challenge is determining which tool or combination of tools should be applied. The following six case studies show how the relevant tools can be selected. The clues that accompany claims can direct you to draw on the appropriate tools. A more philosophical goal of the case studies is to emphasize that it is possible to be a critic without being a cynic. Cynics tend to take an all-or-nothing approach to accepting or rejecting information. In contrast, good critical reasoners carefully separate the possible truths from the likely untruths and have rationales for rejecting the untruths. In this way, they prepare themselves for the next set of claims on a particular issue. If new evidence comes to light, it is easier to reconcile conflicting evidence with a viewpoint that leaves room for nuance than with a more cynical, black-and-white perspective.

Case 1: chemicals, crops, and cancer

The claim

Glyphosate—an herbicide that is applied to the many crops that have been genetically engineered to withstand it—has been linked to non-Hodgkin's lymphoma—cancer of white blood cells.

The stakeholder making the claim

The statement was made in an article that painted a negative picture about genetically engineered food. The article appeared in the magazine of a major environmental organization in July 2001.

The clues

The article does not cite any evidence to support the link. Proving that exposure to a chemical causes a disease is very challenging, especially because other potentially confounding factors may distinguish the people exposed to and not exposed to the chemical. Also, if good evidence suggested that a commonly used pesticide caused a significant increase in cancer cases, the story should have run in the mainstream media. Finally, even if the link could be proven, it would not be a good argument against genetically engineered crops unless the pesticides used on conventional crops were shown to be safer than glyphosate.

The caveat

From a search of the scientific literature available at the time the claim was made, the claim appears to be based on a retrospective epidemiological study. In the study, people were questioned about their exposure to pesticides, and people with non-Hodgkin's lymphoma were compared to those without the disease. In the results section of the original scientific paper, it was reported that four of the people with non-Hodgkin's lymphoma and three of the people without the disease had been exposed to glyphosate. Obviously these numbers are too small to draw conclusions about the dangers of glyphosate; moreover, the researchers say this in their paper.

The conclusions

Even without tracking down the original research paper to evaluate the claim, the available clues—potential bias combined with the lack of evidence about the link between cause and effect—should be sufficient to induce skepticism in someone who has read the previous chapters in this book. Specifically, Chapter 2, "Who's Who?," should leave one suspicious of the source, an environmental organization that tends to be biased in favor of organic agriculture. As a general rule, when newsworthy claims fail to make it into the mainstream media, extra caution is required in interpreting those claims. Chapter 4, "Compare and Contrast," should draw attention to the problem of using a weakness of a technology to dismiss the technology without comparing it to its alternatives. Chapter 5, "What Happens If…?," should make one critical of the ease of linking a complex disease to the exposure to a chemical. To anyone who looks up the original paper, Chapter 7, "Fun Figures," should trigger an additional criticism because the numbers on which the claim is based are clearly too small to be significant. A larger epidemiological study or an experimental study in animals could potentially provide evidence that glyphosate exposure and cancer are linked, but this study does not.

Case 2: the price of smelling fresh

The claim

Frequent underarm shaving in combination with deodorant use might increase a woman's risk of getting breast cancer.

The stakeholder making the claim

The claim was published in a peer-reviewed scientific journal in January 2004.

The clues

The study was based on a survey of the shaving and deodorant use habits of women with breast cancer. It found that the more frequently a woman shaved and applied deodorant, the younger she was when diagnosed with breast cancer. The study did not include a control group of women without breast cancer.

The caveat

In this study, the lack of a control group of women without breast cancer is a giant red flag. It makes it impossible to determine whether more rigorous underarm hygiene causes breast cancer. Perhaps younger women are more likely to shave and apply deodorant than older women. Younger women might be more zealous about underarm care because of changing cultural norms, because they sweat more, or because they more frequently wear clothing that bares their underarms. If the researchers had asked, they likely would have found that the younger women wore makeup and painted their toenails more frequently, but of course they would not claim these habits cause breast cancer. Suggesting a cause and effect relationship between toenail painting and breast cancer seems silly. There must be some other explanation, such as young women wear sandals more often, or just have more time to spend on themselves. By the same logic, the younger women in the group of breast cancer patients could have more rigorous underarm hygiene regimes because they happen to be younger, not because shaving and use of deodorant cause breast cancer. For the link to be more convincing, the researchers would need to show that, in a control group of women without breast cancer, the young women shave and apply deodorant less often than their same age counterparts with breast cancer.

The conclusions

Even claims made in a reliable journal by an expert can be flawed. As discussed in Chapter 5, observational studies often have confounding factors that make them especially vulnerable to being overturned by later studies. To make any connection between breast cancer, deodorant, and shaving, the study would need to be repeated with the appropriate age-matched controls.

Case 3: stormy future

The claim

Hurricane frequency in the North Atlantic is increasing as a result of global warming and elevated sea-surface temperatures. The most intense storms could worsen.

The stakeholder making the claim

The possible link between global warming and hurricane frequency and intensity has been given considerable attention in a wide range of media since Hurricane Katrina hit New Orleans in August 2005.

The clues

Without satellites, hurricanes can be difficult to detect unless they make landfall. Many hurricanes form and peter out over the open ocean. These are much easier to detect with the many weather satellites now dedicated to that purpose. The possibility that the most intense storms may worsen is based on computational modeling. The scientists quoted in the reports are usually cautious about drawing the link between hurricane frequency or intensity and global warming.

The caveat

Although hurricane counts reveal a large jump in the average annual number of hurricanes over the past decade, it is difficult to say for sure whether global warming increases hurricane frequency. The elevated counts could be due to improved hurricane detection. Some researchers also think that hurricane numbers vary cyclically, so even if the elevated counts are real, it may be a cyclic variation, rather than the result of global warming. Current computer models that suggest hurricane intensity may increase are flawed because they have difficulty reproducing large hurricanes in "hindcasts" of past storm seasons.

The conclusions

Based on the process of science discussion in Chapter 1, "Potions, Plot, Personalities," the known limitations of early computational models should create uncertainty regarding potential changes in hurricane intensity. Doubts should also be raised by the discord among scientists regarding the relationship between global warming and hurricane intensity and frequency. In addition, as described in Chapter 7, it makes sense to be skeptical about data when the way of collecting that data may have changed over time, as it has with improvements in storm-tracking technology. However, because warm water is needed to fuel hurricanes, there is a plausible mechanism by which global warming could worsen hurricanes. Therefore, it is certainly possible that more sophisticated computer models and future data collection will provide more solid evidence for the hurricane/global-warming link.

Case 4: discovery of the obesity gene

The claim

The gene for obesity has been discovered. (The same claim has been made at different times for different genes.)

The stakeholder making the claim

This claim has been made in headlines in mainstream media.

The clues

Since the claim makes obesity sound very simple, it should raise several questions. Could it really be true that one gene is responsible for the obesity epidemic? What about diet? What about exercise? In recent decades, as obesity has become more prevalent, has there been a change in humans' genetic makeup?

The caveat

It is common to read claims that the gene for this or that disorder has been discovered. However, neither nature (genes) nor nurture (environment) is solely responsible for variation between individuals. Virtually all traits are the result of an interaction between genes and the environment.

The conclusions

As discussed in Chapter 1, the media often simplifies science to create eye-catching headlines. As discussed in Chapter 5, multiple interacting causes are the norm in diseases and many other phenomena. Finally, as discussed in Chapter 6, "Specific or General," a factor that plays a critical role for one group of people may not play the same role for another. The so-called gene for obesity very likely plays some role in metabolism or weight maintenance, but it is not the only gene involved, and environment and lifestyle also play a role. This will be the case nearly every time you read the headline "Gene for X Discovered," where X is the condition *du jour*.

Case 5: clear and current danger

The claim

Many claims have been made about the electric and magnetic fields (EMF) that exist close to electrical appliances and lines that carry electrical currents. According to the claims, these fields can cause nausea, headaches, fatigue, muscle pain, and even cancer. One specific claim is that EMF is classified as a Group 2B carcinogen by the International Agency for Research on Cancer (IARC) of the World Health Organization (WHO), and that DDT and lead are also classified as Group 2B carcinogens.

The stakeholder making the claim

The claim about EMF as a Group 2B carcinogen was made in a brochure advertising chips and pendants that supposedly counteract the effects of EMF.

The clues

Clearly the stakeholder making the claim has something to gain by convincing people that EMF is dangerous. Therefore, the claim should elicit two questions. Is EMF really a Group 2B carcinogen? What does it really mean for something to be classified as a Group 2B carcinogen?

The caveat

The IARC does classify EMF as a Group 2B carcinogen. The IARC's categories are: 1) carcinogenic to humans; 2A) probably carcinogenic to humans; 2B) possibly carcinogenic to humans; 3) not classifiable as to carcinogenicity in humans; and 4) probably not carcinogenic to humans. Lead and DDT are also in Group 2B, but so are gasoline, pickled vegetables, and coffee.

The conclusions

The claim about the carcinogenicity of EMF exploits a quirk in our reasoning processes discussed in Chapter 9, "All the Tricks in the Book." We have the tendency to overgeneralize. We know that lead was banned from paint and gasoline, and DDT was banned from being sprayed on crops, so we conclude that if EMF is in the same category, it must be dangerous. However, neither lead nor DDT was banned because it was proven to cause cancer. Lead was banned because it can damage nerve connections, especially in young children. DDT was banned because it impairs eggshell quality in birds at the top of the food chain. The evidence that lead and DDT cause cancer is weak, as is the evidence that EMF causes cancer. A task group convened by the WHO concluded that the electric fields generally encountered by the public do not pose any substantive health risks. The WHO also rejected the adoption of EMF exposure limits, but encouraged the exploration of low-cost methods of reducing exposure, a recommendation consistent with a costs-benefits analysis rather than the precautionary principle (as defined in Chapter 8, "Society's Say").

Case 6: diet debacle

The claim
"Low-fat diet cuts health risks? Fat Chance."

The stakeholder making the claim
The claim was the headline of an article from *The New York Times* News Service and the *Washington Post* that made the front page of newspapers across the country in February 2006.

The clues
The first part of the article was consistent with the headline. It described an eight-year study in which women were randomly selected to follow a low-fat diet or to not change their diet. The article reported that the experimental (low fat) group did not have a lower risk of heart attack, stroke, colon cancer, or breast cancer than the control group. However, the real story is revealed by clues buried deep within the article. The women in the experimental group decreased their fat intake by approximately 10 percent, which was not as great a reduction as the researchers were hoping the women would achieve. Nonetheless, these women had slightly lower blood pressure, LDL, or "bad," cholesterol, as well as slightly fewer colon polyps than the women in the control group. Although breast cancer risk did not differ significantly between the two groups, there was a trend suggesting that the low-fat diet was associated with reduced risk. The researchers speculated that the trend might become significant if followed over a longer time.

The caveat

It is common to see headlines, especially about health issues, essentially proclaiming that everything you know is wrong. The first half of the article goes on to support the headline, but if you are motivated enough to follow the story to the jump page, you will often find that the second half of the story contradicts the first half. A more honest headline for this particular story would be: "Modest cut in fat intake, modest health benefits." Yawn. Obviously, that would not sell newspapers.

The conclusions

This is another example of the problem described in Chapter 1 in which a headline simplifies a complex story to sensationalize it. After all, there were health benefits, albeit small, of the sort-of-low-fat diet. Furthermore, as discussed in Chapter 3, it is misleading to create a black-and-white choice from something that is more complex. The headline and first half of the story ignored the fact that reducing total fat in the diet is not the only alteration that can be made to fat intake. It is also important to consider the type of fat in the diet (for example, saturated fat, unsaturated fat, trans fat). Finally, as discussed in Chapter 6, it is incorrect to assume that a study carried out with one group (in this case, women aged 50 to 79) would hold up in other groups, or that a study carried out over one time frame (in this case, eight years) would have the same results as a longer study. Ironically, all these nuances are mentioned in the article, but only a reader motivated enough to follow the story to the jump page would find them. A good rule of thumb for approaching articles that look like they overturn reasonably well-accepted health information is to skim the first part of the article, and then search the second part of the article for explicit contradictions.

Information sleuthing

As the case studies illustrate, reasoning critically does not have to take more time than absorbing information passively. They are simply different ways of processing information. However, the case studies also show that sometimes it is helpful to do additional research. While no one has the time to research the specifics of each of the new claims that bombard us daily, anytime you find yourself using such information to make decisions about your life—like what to buy, how to vote, what to eat, and how to spend your leisure time—it pays to get the facts straight and put claims in perspective. Sleuthing involves tracing information back to its source to see whether it has been accurately represented, or searching for related information to provide a more complete view of the issue. The tools discussed in *Lies, Damned Lies, and Science* facilitate the sleuthing process by revealing the gaps in understanding that need to be filled. For example, after reading a study that links a cause and effect, you may want to know whether there are any studies that examine potential confounding factors, or whether the relationship between cause and effect has been studied in other groups or under other conditions. Alternatively, you may determine that you need to actively seek out information about a theme of tradeoff, such as long-term health risks, that seems to have been overlooked.

Bunk busters

Debunking the most rampant or egregious claims may not require much sleuthing because someone may have already done the work for you. Snopes (www.snopes.com), About Urban Legends (http://urbanlegends. about.com), and Break the Chain (http://breakthechain.org) can help debunk those annoying fear stories passed along by friends and acquaintances. Sense About Science (www.senseaboutscience.org) is dedicated to responding to inaccuracies in public claims and includes a section on the many bogus claims made by celebrities. Improving Medical Statistics (www.improvingmedicalstatistics.com/) provides a helping hand with identifying potentially flawed data in health studies. The *Skeptical Inquirer* (www.csicop.org/si) tackles a variety of topics with the goal of separating science from pseudoscience.

Like a blood hound

Bunk busters do not catch all of the bogus information that is out there because there is an awful lot of it. Determining whether information has come down the lines of a "broken telephone" may require tracking the information back to its source. As discussed in Chapter 2, the latest scientific advances are often made public via a press release written by someone at the home institution of the study's principle author. Good science journalists use the press release as a heads up, and as a basis for building their story, but they talk to the scientist directly, and perhaps others in the field, and provide additional context in their story. Even the most accurate press release tends to spin the science a little to make it seem more exciting to entice journalists (who receive loads of press releases) into reporting on the discovery. Therefore, a carefully crafted news story can do a more accurate and balanced job of representing the science than the original press release. However, too often, rushed reporters base their stories nearly entirely on the press release. Even worse, to make it their own, simplify it, or make it more attention grab-bing, they tweak it just enough that it becomes incorrect. Other reporters may create their own stories based on the incorrect version. One time I sent out a press release in which the name of a scientist (who had an unusual moniker) kept morphing as the story was picked up by one careless reporter after another, each incorporating the previous error and adding another.

Tracking down an original press release is straightforward. It will be posted on the news Web site of the principle author's home institution. Other Web sites, including EurekAlert! (www.eurekalert.org), Science Daily (www.sciencedaily.com), and Medical News Today (www.medical-newstoday.com), post press releases from around the world on a daily basis, and maintain archives of past press releases. Of course, a press release is not as reliable as a peer-reviewed source, so it is useful to track down the original scientific paper on which the press release is based. The search engine Google Scholar (http://scholar.google.com) simplifies the process enormously. Type in the relevant keywords including the science topic, authors' names, name of the scientific journal in which the original piece was published, or as much of this information as you have been able to glean from the news article. Restrict the search to recent articles if relevant. Google Scholar provides direct links to the online ver-sions of journal articles. The abstract—short summary—of the article is available to anyone, but depending on the journal, access to the full arti-cle may be open only to members. The abstract is often sufficient to determine whether the science has been distorted in the press release or news story. If the abstract is not sufficiently informative, and the journal article is not available for free, it will be accessible through a computer at a university library if the university subscribes to those journals. Fortu-nately, since not everyone lives close to a university, more and more jour-nals are making their articles freely available online within six months to a year after being published.

Is it peer reviewed?

Google Scholar is much more user friendly and easily accessible than the many science databases. However, not all of the articles it picks up are peer-reviewed. Peer-reviewed articles have a reference section with references that look something like this:

Seethaler, S. & Linn, M. (2004). Genetically modified food in perspective: An inquiry-based curriculum to help middle school students make sense of tradeoffs. *International Journal of Science Education,* 26 (14), 1765-1785.

Not surprisingly, unscrupulous stakeholders sometimes mimic this style to make it appear that their work has been peer-reviewed. So it is important to determine where the research has been published. A partial list of peer-reviewed science journals can be found on EurekAlert! (www.eurekalert.org/links.php).

Checking all the angles

Scientific papers tend to be full of terminology and rather remarkable cures for insomnia. While many are accessible to motivated nonscientists, some really are only completely comprehensible to other scientists in the same field. Therefore, it is often necessary to rely on secondary sources—those written by someone other than the researchers who performed the study—that have not been peer reviewed. *Scientific American, Discover Magazine, New Scientist, Popular Science, Popular Mechanics, Science News,* The Why Files, NPR Science Friday, and BBC Science and Nature are some of the popular science magazines, radio and television shows, and Web sites that do a good job of presenting and analyzing science. Some academic journals, such as *Science, Nature,* and *Journal of the American Medical Association,* also have articles and commentaries written for nonspecialists. Many universities have educational Web sites on different science topics, which can be good sources of information. For controversial issues, Wikipedia—the free online encyclopedia—can be a good place to begin gathering information from multiple sources. The advantage of Wikipedia is that it usually provides different perspectives on an issue and includes linked references, which can be followed up easily.

The Web sites of national and international government agencies and organizations often have extensive resources for the public. Examples include health information from the World Health Organization, U.S. National Institutes of Health, and U.S. Centers for Disease Control and Prevention; information about the environment/natural resources from the Intergovernmental Panel on Climate Change, U.S. Environmental Protection Agency, and U.S. Department of Agriculture; and coverage of space sciences from the European Space Agency and the National Aeronautics and Space Administration. Some Web sites facilitate one-stop-shopping because they link to a wide range of resources. For example, the U.S. National Institutes of Health Web site (www.nih.gov) has reader-friendly articles and newsletters, information about research funding, and links to databases of peer-reviewed health research papers (PubMed), drug information (Medline Plus), and international clinical trials looking for participants to test cutting-edge treatments and preventative strategies for many diseases and disorders (http://clinicaltrials.gov).

Think tanks—organizations that advocate positions on specific issues and conduct research—are another source of information. The number of think tanks around the world has exploded in recent decades. Think tanks are funded by government, industry, or philanthropic organizations, and represent a variety of ideologies. The analyses provided by different think tanks can be useful in identifying the range of possible tradeoffs of an innovation or policy. However, think tanks' political leanings may bias their findings, so they cannot be trusted as a sole source of information. Of course, government sources can also be distorted by political leanings. For example, U.S. government agencies have been pressured to toe the line on abstinence-only sex education and climate change. Although any source of information may be biased, particularly unreliable sources of information are those written by people who have no science background and who do not consult with scientists. For example, popular celebrity/fashion/heath magazines often perpetuate myths and half-truths, especially about diet and nutrition. Tracing information back to its source, considering perspectives from across the political spectrum, looking at the media from other countries, and considering the information presented by different types of organizations are all useful options for checking out the different angles of an issue.

In science class, we were expected to read or listen with the goal of absorbing information like a sponge. In contrast, becoming a good critical reasoner entails adding a quality-control filter to process information, and taking a more active approach to integrating the information that passes through the filter. With practice, the flaws in news stories and stakeholders' arguments start to jump out. It becomes second nature to judge whether a claim is adequately supported by the evidence presented. Brainstorming potential confounds becomes a reflex to hearing about a purported link between cause and effect. Claims about scientific consensus, disputes, or undiscovered scientific genius call out to be scrutinized with respect to relevant features of the scientific process. The big picture context and ignored options become more readily perceptible. Biased assessments of risks and benefits become transparent. Stakeholders' ploys to bypass logic fail. But like the Matryoshka dolls, scientific issues do not automatically reveal their intricacies. Only when you know what to look for will you find what you need to make balanced decisions. That is the power of the tools that formed the basis of each chapter. The conclusions summarize the major applications of the ten tools in a handy, easily referenced format.

Conclusion: twenty essential applications of the tools

Understand how science progresses and why scientists sometimes disagree

1. Legitimate criticism can be distinguished from science bashing.

Those who poke fun at science because it is incomplete, uncertain, and tentative either utterly misunderstand what science is, or are misrepresenting it to promote their own agendas. It is legitimate to identify gaps and inconsistencies in knowledge to point out where more work needs to be done, or to call for caution in interpreting findings, but uncertainty is not a reason to simply dismiss the scientific research.

2. Claims about scientific disputes or consensus should not be taken at face value.

Since science is a work in progress, it is natural for scientists to disagree about the interpretation of research findings. Stakeholders, including the media, commonly sweep scientists' disagreements under the rug to make things appear simpler than they are. At other times, they create the illusion that the scientific community is evenly divided on an issue, when the vast majority of scientists have come to a consensus.

3. Beware of the self-declared revolutionary who claims to be unappreciated by the scientific community.

Scientists do not work in complete isolation and undiscovered genius is rare. Although there are historical examples of ideas being overlooked because they were before their time, self-proclaimed revolutionaries usually turn out to be hucksters, or at least barking up the wrong tree. Peer review is a key step in the progress of science, and ideas that have not survived peer review should be treated with healthy skepticism.

Identify those who hold stake in an issue and what their positions are

4. Bias is everywhere.

People have many reasons for trying to convince you of their point of view, or at least catch your attention. Even when stakeholders are genuinely trying to be objective, their unconscious biases will shape the way they select and interpret information.

5. Return to the initial source and seek the perspectives of a range of stakeholders.

As information passes between successive sources, it often becomes increasingly distorted. Therefore, when possible, it is useful to trace ideas back to their origin. It is also helpful to unearth the voices of stakeholders with different perspectives on an issue (for example, the rich, the poor, vendors, consumers, politicians, regulatory agencies, environmentalists, industry representatives, academics, and so on).

Elucidate all the pros and cons of a decision

6. The apparent choices are often false dichotomies.

Despite the oversimplification and polarization of the choices with which we are presented, there are usually multiple alternatives. A decision is only sound if it takes into account each of the options, including the *status quo*.

7. The list of risks and benefits presented is usually incomplete.

The risks and benefits of a decision may involve the environment, the economy, human health and well-being, and ethics. Each risk or benefit may be long term, short term, or both. Rarely do individual stakeholders explore all the themes of risks and benefits.

8. Each application of an innovation has a unique set of risks and benefits.

Even if the risks outweigh the benefits for one application of a technology or policy, other uses of the same innovation may fare favorably in the risks-benefits analysis.

Place alternatives in an appropriate context to evaluate tradeoffs

9. The bigger picture provides a reference point for considering options.

It is easy to be misled by the omission of an appropriate context for comparison, such as alternative technologies, policies implemented in other regions, or outcomes that occurred in a similar situation in the past. Numbers are especially tricky unless they are considered in an appropriate context or re-expressed to expose their real meaning.

10. Pointing to weaknesses in a competing idea is not the same as proving the proposed alternative is the best option.

Since each alternative has weaknesses and benefits, simply expounding the weaknesses of one option does not prove it should be abandoned. The weaknesses of the alternatives must also be scrutinized.

Distinguish between cause and coincidence

11. Confounds make it difficult to determine the cause of something.

Anecdotes are often presented as "proof" that one thing caused another, but just because something preceded an occurrence does not mean it was the cause. With a little brainstorming, it is usually possible to come up with several plausible causes. For complex issues, multiple interacting causes are common.

12. "Blind" trials are very important for protecting against bias.

Our expectations color our perceptions and can even affect our health. For this reason, placebos are critical in health studies. In any field, there is a risk that inadvertent or deliberate bias will be introduced when the person collecting the data is aware which condition is the control and which is the experimental.

13. Combining multiple forms of data can help confirm a link between cause and effect.

All types of studies have inherent weaknesses. Therefore, when data from different studies (epidemiological/observational, experimental, modeling) point to the same cause, there is a greater probability that it is the cause. The link between cause and effect is also more likely if there is a plausible mechanism that could link them.

Recognize how broadly conclusions from a study may be applied

14. Findings from one situation frequently fail to hold up in other situations.

The results of a study may be influenced by the characteristics of the population being studied, the location at which the study is carried out, the prevailing conditions, and the length of the study.

See through the number jumble

15. The meaning of statistics can be distorted by the data collection procedures.

Selection bias can arise when poll respondents or experimental subjects are not chosen randomly. Changes in the way data are collected can result in a statistical change even when there has been no genuine change in circumstances over time.

16. Numbers cannot be taken at face value.

Not all statistical differences are significant and/or meaningful. Apparent trends often arise because of natural fluctuations in data. Hidden confounding factors can lead to a statistical relationship between two factors even when a real relationship does not exist.

Discern the relationships between science and policy

17. When results cannot be reconciled, the truth is often somewhere in the middle.

Social factors influence what science gets done, how it gets done, and how it is interpreted. When results touted by different groups are hopelessly conflicted, reality is likely to be well within the two extremes, unless one group has a stronger vested interest than the other and is presenting less, or lower-quality scientific evidence.

18. A costs benefits analysis is the most systematic method of decision-making.

The precautionary principle is a popular basis for policy decisions, but, unlike a costs benefits analysis, the precautionary principle fails to take all the risks and benefits of all the alternatives into account.

Get past the ploys designed to simply bypass logic

19. Familiarity with the weaknesses in your own reasoning processes makes you more resistant to efforts to manipulate you.

People often have trouble reasoning outside the box, jump to conclusions about cause and effect, overgeneralize, and listen more carefully to ideas that confirm their beliefs while tuning out ideas that contradict them. People also tend to abandon logic in favor of emotions and gut reactions in the face of cleverly designed persuasive messages.

Know how to seek information to gain a balanced perspective

20. Many layers of understanding become apparent through the exploration of an issue.

Peeling back the layers of a science-related issue is facilitated by knowing what to look for (as discussed in this book) and consulting a range of types of sources of information.

Acknowledgments

Writing a book is a journey of faith and love, not just on the part of the author, but also on the part of everyone who helps make it happen, including those whose roles were played long before the journey began. Without my mom, I wouldn't be here. I realize I have an amazing grasp of the obvious, but she really is the best mom anyone could hope to have. My grandpa, Bill, although he had little formal education, taught me about nature and instilled in me a sense of curiosity about the natural world that lives on to this day.

Throughout my life I have been blessed with wonderful teachers and mentors who have given me incredible opportunities, believed in me, and encouraged me to follow my dreams. To name just one from each phase of my life from high school to present—Sharon McKenna, Judith Poë, Haig Keshishian, Jacques Prim, Marcia Linn, and Kim McDonald challenged me to think hard, love science, write better, and believe in myself.

In the People's Republic of Berkeley, I met the most interesting, stimulating people who broadened my horizons and didn't let me take myself too seriously. Tim Zimmerman, Chris Moore, Chris Wu, Ming Ho, Ernie Lo, Carole Newlands, and Stephanie Sisk-Hilton all told me I could do it and shared my insatiable desire for Thai food.

This book would never have been published without my wonderful agent Jodie Rhodes, who was not afraid to take on something a little bit different, and who worked tenaciously to find me a home. The folks at FT Press Science have such extraordinary vision, and I especially want to thank Amanda Moran for helping me negotiate the publication process, and Russ Hall for his thoughtful editorial feedback. I am also extremely grateful to the editors, especially Alan Rinzler, who could not take the book, but provided insightful feedback that shaped it and made it stronger. Thank you also to April Maskiewicz for her feedback on an early draft.

Finally, I am eternally indebted to Barbara Sawrey, who made me laugh the most along this journey. Everyone needs a wonderwall, and she's mine.

Words have extraordinary power. Choose them carefully, and use them wisely.

About the Author

Sherry Seethaler, a science writer and educator at the University of California, San Diego, works with scientists to explain their discoveries to the public. She also writes a column for the *San Diego Union-Tribune* answering readers' questions about science. Seethaler holds an M.S. and Master of Philosophy in biology from Yale, and a Ph.D. in science and math education from UC Berkeley.

Index